"ᛦᚾᚠᛖᛋ? Runes."

A comprehensive workbook and reference guide to The Elder Futhark, Younger Futhark, and the Futhorc as well as an introduction to the Runic Mysticism that is Bind Runes.

Featuring original poetry, divinatory meanings, examples and perspectives that are my own personal interpretations and creations that I have learned and built upon as I continue to deepen my relationship with the energies, and spirits we call the Runes.

I do wish to acknowledge some amazing authors that I've been able to know and recommend over the years: Kenn Edwards and the book "Rune Walker," Siri Vincent-Plouff with "Queering the Runes," Sophia Fate-Changer with "The Language of Fire and Ice," Ryan Smith and "The Way of Fire and Ice," and James Calico who continues to provide theoretical, oftentimes realized rabbit holes based on historical and archeological evidence.

This book, like all my works, is dedicated to my children, Benjamin, Annaleia, and Emmett, my partners in crime, and fellow trouble makers; and to my amazing wife, without whose support, love and care I would be lost.

I also wish to thank my friends and chosen family for their counsel, advice, and support as well. and all of my dearest kin, especially Asra, the very best editor and a true confidant.

It is my desire that this book help all who search out the meanings and powers of the Runes, and that they discover the energies that make up the Runes. May you all thrive in your path of learning, knowledge, history, cultures, and the reason you're here:
the Runes.
-Liagis

A Preface of Sorts:

The goal of this book is to bring The Elder Futhark, The Younger Futhark and the Futhorc together in a fashion that is easy to navigate, to study, to make notes, and to adapt to one's practice. In my eyes this is best accomplished by placing each section with like or similar Runes together so as to make comparisons and quick references easier on the reader. In addition to these sections you will find note sheets for your own reflection after each cohort of Runes, as well as nine workbook pages to make your own Bind Runes at the end of the Bind Rune section. Then to wrap up the book, you will also find thirteen workbook pages to keep monthly Rune reading notes on.

The way I recommend taking advantage of the workbook pages after each Rune cohort is to stop on the rune you're drawn to, and then either draw the rune on a medium, hold the rune in your hand from your set, or mentally picture it. From here, spend time with it, speak to it, meditate with it, and as you make a connection with it, record your findings in the workbook pages.

You will also notice that there isn't an exhaustive source page at the end of this. That's because, true to my word, most of this book is from my learned experience and personal practice. However I do wish to give due credit to Ann Groa Sheffield and their book "Long Branches of the Younger Futhark," Kenn Edwards mentioned previously and Alaric Albertsson with "Saxon Sorcery and Magic" for their amazing work and research on the lesser discussed Younger Futhark and the Futhorc. I'd also like to give credit as an invaluable source to Ragweedforge.com, the source of the rune poems listed near the end of the book.

This book is divination focused first, and there's a couple reasons for this. The first is that it's what the community needs. This is my effort to bring my knowledge, in my style and in an accessible manner, to the larger Heathen, Pagan, and other spiritual communities. The second is that it is through divination and working with the runes that beings begin to build their relationship with the runes, which allows them to dig deeper and build their craft or path. With divination being mentioned (and a pretty big deal in this book), it's worth mentioning too that context is everything when it comes to a cast, pull, or reading. Just because a rune comes up reversed doesn't mean it's the end of the world; look to the rest of the reading to inform that process. The same can be said if every rune comes out upright. Let the read and the runes dictate the context and guidance given. If you have two readings of the same runes and you get the same answer, you're not truly listening.

All runes will be listed in order from Elder Futhark, Younger Futhark, and then the Futhorc; this is the case for the names, the rune shapes and the pronunciations. You will also notice I have only included magical correspondences for each rune section on more positive connotations. I am not against cursing, or hexing, and practice it myself, but it is not my place to say that you should or should not, nor do I want to divulge that part of my practice at this time. These correspondences are not exhaustive either, merely a stepping stone for you to dive deeper into the craft.

Now to switch gears: yes I do use the blank rune because, although it was invented by someone for capitalistic gain, it acquired a new significance in the eyes and hands of many Rune crafters, including mine. This is not to say everyone should use it, or should not use it. I am merely stating why I do. I am not a reconstructionist, or someone who thinks the only way to do things is the safe and established way; I believe in and follow in the agency and energies of the Rúnvættir, Wyrd, and the divine that follow.

Another big change that the reader will notice is that I do not subscribe to the idea of referring to the Futhorc Runic System as the Anglo-Saxon Futhorc. This is due to the fact that the term refers to a time that historians study prior to 1066 and and has no need of being used after that date. The terms more often used by scholars are either Anglo-Frisian Futhorc, or Early/Old English Futhorc[1]. Due to this you will see me refer to this system simply as the Futhorc throughout the book.

---

[1] https://www.academia.edu/33256399/On_the_Origin_of_the_Anglo_Frisian_runic_Innovations

Foreword

By Travis Wells

Language is one of the greatest powers gifted to humankind, a tool that bridges the chasm between thought and reality. It shapes worlds, binds communities, and weaves the threads of history into stories that endure through the ages. In the Norse lore, it was Odin who first grasped the runes, sacrificing himself to the windswept branches of Yggdrasil to wrest their secrets from the void. Through this act of will and sacrifice, the Allfather gifted not just a system of symbols but the very essence of language's power: to name, to know, and to create.

The runes are far more than mere marks upon stone or wood; they are whispers of ancient wisdom, bearers of mysteries older than memory. In their embrace lies a journey—one that transcends the boundaries of time and space, connecting you to the realms of gods, men, and the threads of your own spirit. To walk the path of the runes is to tread a road of spirit and song, of seeking and becoming—a journey for those who dare to listen to the voices within the symbols.

I consider Liagis kinfolk, not by blood but by the bond forged through shared devotion to sacred craft. Their counsel has not only guided me through the labyrinth of runic knowledge but has also emboldened me to trust my intuition and honor the wisdom of my own lived experience. In this work, they have woven together threads of lore and intuition into a tapestry both sturdy and beautiful—a gift to all who would take up the work of the runes.

Within these pages lies a careful melding of scholarly wisdom and personal practice. Like a craftsperson who tempers steel with fire, the author draws upon sources of venerable age and their own hard-won insights, forging a tool both practical and profound. The arrangement of runes into their kindred groups, the space for reflection and creation, and the gentle counsel offered throughout all serve to make this book more than a reference. It is a companion, a mentor, and a mirror to your own personal practice.

Liagis has rooted this work in divination, for it is through such practice that the runes awaken to us. In their casting, drawing, and meditating, one learns to listen—to hear the voices of the Runes, to feel the threads of Wyrd as they twist and weave through the present. It is a sacred dialogue, one that teaches us more of ourselves than of any potential future.

But this book is no tyrant of tradition, no rigid keeper of one "true" way. It grants the reader freedom to explore, to question, and to grow. The premise here is clear: the practitioner must form a direct personal relationship with the runes to truly unlock their potential. Presented here not as relics of a bygone era but as living companions, the runes await those who seek their counsel.

If you have ever felt the ancient call of the sacred within you—a pull toward the mysteries of the runes—then this book will guide you on that path. May you walk with the runes, learn their ways, and find in their wisdom the courage to navigate the great tapestry of life.

Table of Contents

Pg. 8. The Rune sets
Pg. 9. The Origin of the Runes
Pg. 13. The Aetts of The Elder Futhark
Pg. 17. Fehu, Fé, Feoh
Pg. 22. Uruz, Úr, Ur
Pg. 28. Thurisaz, Thurs, þorn
Pg. 33. Ansuz, As, Os
Pg. 38. Raidho. Reið, Rad
Pg. 43. Kenaz, Kaun, Ken
Pg. 48. Gebo, Gifu
Pg. 52. Wunjo, Wyn
Pg. 57. Hagalaz, Hagall, Hegel
Pg. 62. Nauthiz, Nauðr, Nyd
Pg. 67. Isa, Ísa, Is
Pg. 73 . Jera, Ár, Ger
Pg. 78. Eihwaz, Yr, Eoh/Yr
Pg. 84. Perthro, Peorth
Pg. 88. Algiz, Eolh
Pg. 92. Sowilo, Söl, Sigel
Pg. 98. Tiwaz, Tyr, Tiw
Pg. 103. Berkano, Björk, Beorc
Pg. 108. Ehwaz, Eh
Pg. 112. Mannaz, Maðr, Man
Pg. 117. Laguz, Lögr, Lagu
Pg. 122. Ingwaz, Ing
Pg. 126. Dagaz, Dæg
Pg. 130. Othala, Eþel
Pg. 134. The Last of the Futhorc
Pg. 135. Ac, Æsc
Pg. 139. Ear, Calc
Pg. 143. Gar
Pg. 145. The Source Rune
Pg. 147. My Rune Poem
Pg. 149. The Historical Rune Poems
Pg. 157. Bind Runes
Pg. 183. The Galdr Chants
Pg. 187. Runic Divination
Pg. 202. The Runes: A Recount
Pg. 204 The Author

The Elder Futhark

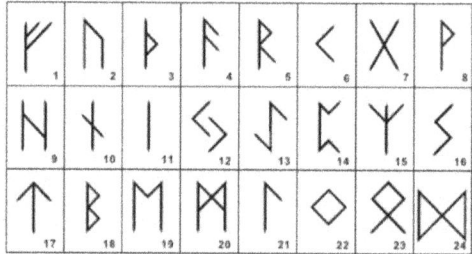

The Younger Futhark

The Futhorc

The Origin of The Runes

Man's Recording of the Runes:

The history behind the origin and creation of the runes as we know them is twofold: the version recorded by man in history, and the darker retelling of how the Allfather Odin brought them into being.

The runes are presumed to have been derived from one of the many Old Italic alphabets in use among the Mediterranean peoples of the first century CE, who lived to the south of the Germanic tribes. Earlier Germanic sacred symbols, such as those preserved in northern European carvings, were also likely influential in the development of this systemic alphabet.

The earliest possibly runic inscription that we know of is found on the Meldorf brooch, which was manufactured in the north of modern-day Germany around 50 CE. The inscription is highly ambiguous, however, and scholars are divided over whether its letters are Runic or Roman. The earliest unambiguous runic inscriptions are found on the Vimose comb from Vimose, Denmark and the Ovre Stabu spearhead from southern Norway, both of which date to approximately 160 CE. The earliest known carving of the entire futhark, in order, is that on the Kylver stone from Gotland, Sweden, which dates to roughly 400 CE. This was the situation as it stood in 2021, when the Svingerud Stone was discovered and was radiocarbon dated to have been made between 1 and 250 CE, making it the world's oldest runic inscription.[2]

The transmission of writing from region to region in Europe likely took place via Germanic warbands, the dominant northern European military of this period, who would have encountered Italic writing firsthand during campaigns amongst their southerly neighbors. This hypothesis is supported by the association that Runes have always had with the god Odin, who, in the Proto-Germanic period under his original name Wodan, was the divine model of the human warband leader and the invisible patron of the warband's activities. The Roman historian Tacitus tells us that Odin, also known as Mercury to the Romans, was already established as the dominant god in the pantheons of many of the Proto Germanic tribes by the first century.[3]

Then came the Younger:
The Younger Futhark was first found in conjunction with Elder Futhark on the Rok Runestone dated to the early ninth century.[4] Popularized during what's considered the Viking Age, it's

---

[2] https://ivaldisonsforge.com/blog/432-part-ii-the-origins-of-the-runes.html?srsltid=AfmBOorF1lcjN4ng6viwzLk1LkFvubw7Ll0iJb30i7T37EhS332e_Yhh
[3] https://en.wikipedia.org/wiki/Early_Germanic_culture
[4] https://oldnorse.org/what-are-runes/?srsltid=AfmBOooF9IXcFEbE6nGcf2tA0tRXBIUTVB5NhHQX-QhOj75UuYxx8we1

what most Rune crafters used for writing, which hearkens back to its first usage as being shorthand for sailors and tradespeople. The change was further impacted by the language of the many regions constantly developing: vowels being dropped, words were being shortened, and even the pronunciations of the runes themselves were changing! So when used for writing shortened words in a changing language, that makes it easier to use, right? Actually it was the opposite. Besides being used side by side with the Elder until the mid tenth century, it came with its own unique, and confusing spelling rules due to the number of runes being reduced to sixteen. With some runes representing various sounds with the same spelling, it became a game of intellect at times. Not to mention the Younger Futhark had three distinct styles: Long Branch, Short Branch, and Rodless. These still functioned the same, which threw another wrench (or chisel) into the mix.

How can we use the Younger Futhark in our practice today? Just like its Elder counterpart, each Rune has been attributed a meaning, and epithet all its own which makes it still suitable for Runic magic, such as Galdr or Bindrunes, as well as divinatory purposes, and my favorite for this system - spell composition. Where the Elder is all about the power and energy of the magic in each Rune, the Younger showcases the power of the Runes written into speech and are perfectly adapted for such, especially if one decides to include the additional vowel sounds into their practice.

From Futhark to Futhorc:

Now it's time for a skip and a jump geographically back in time (wibbly, wobbly anyone?) to the fifth century realm of Early England. The Futhorc was first found to be used as early as the third century with its prime usage between the fourth and sixth centuries as the precursor to the Latin alphabet's taking its reign (evident in the changing from Futhark to Futhorc due to the "K" sound Rune changing letters) of immortality. The Futhorc first incorporated 28 runes, instead of the 24 runes of the Elder Futhark. It then became even larger, developing into the full 30-character Futhorc, around the end of the fifth century. This time a changing language on the part of the English made for a Runic system better suited for grammatical writing and record keeping, as well as charms and magical workings - the perfect precursor to the Latin alphabet.[5] Now for the fun stuff.

Odin's Discovery of the Runes:

At the center of the Norse cosmos stands the great tree Yggdrasil. Yggdrasil's upper branches cradle Asgard, the home and fortress of the Aesir gods and goddesses, of whom Odin is the chief.

Yggdrasil's roots grow out of the Well of Urd, a pool whose bottomless abyss holds many of the most powerful forces and beings in the cosmos. Among them are the Norns, Urd, Verandi, and Skuld (what is, becoming, and debt). One of the foremost techniques they use to shape fate is carving the names they choose in Runes amongst stone tablets. The runes then

---

[5] https://www.omniglot.com/writing/futhorc.htm

carry these intentions throughout the tree, and surrounding realms, affecting everything in the Nine Realms.[6]

In my early days of practice this is how I saw the story of Odin gaining the knowledge of the Runes. Odin watched the Norns from his seat in Asgard and envied their powers and their wisdom. Knowing he would be sated only by further knowledge, he bent his will toward the task of coming to know the Runes.

Since the Runes' native home is in the Well of Urd with the Norns, and since the Runes do not reveal themselves to any but those who prove themselves worthy of such fearful insights and abilities, Odin decided to go through the ordeal of hanging himself from a branch of Yggdrasil, pierced his own side with his spear, and peered downward into the shadowy waters below. He forbade any of the other gods to grant him the slightest aid, not even a sip of water, and he stared downward, chasing the depths ever deeper peering into the black as he called to the Runes.

He survived in this state, teetering on the precipice that separates the living from the dead, for no less than nine days and nights. At the end of the ninth night, he at last perceived shapes in the depths: the Runes! They had accepted his sacrifice and shown themselves to him, revealing to him not only their forms, but also the secrets that lie within them. Having fixed this knowledge in his formidable memory, Odin ended his ordeal with a scream of exultation. Having been initiated into the mysteries of the runes, Odin recounted:

"I know I was hanged on the windy tree For nine full nights, Stabbed by a spear, offered to Odin Sworn by myself to myself, Upon that tree that no man knows From what roots it rises. No bread did they bear to me nor horn handed; Into the deep I gazed— I took up the runes, took them up, screaming, Then fell back again. ("Hávamál": 138-39 Carolyne Larrington)

Equipped with the knowledge of how to wield the runes, he became one of the mightiest and most accomplished beings in the cosmos. He learned chants that enabled him to heal emotional and bodily wounds, to bind his enemies and render their weapons worthless, to free himself from constraints, to put out fires, to expose and banish practitioners of malevolent magic, to protect his friends in battle, to wake the dead, to win and keep a lover, and to perform many other feats such as these.

This retelling is found in the Hávamál, an Old Norse poem that comprises part of the Poetic Edda, and is in layman's terms, somewhat of a "How to Heathen Guide." In the first of the two verses that describe Odin's Seidr initiatory ordeal in itself, the Allfather says that he was "given to Odin, myself to myself."[7] The Old Norse phrase that translates to English as

---

[6] https://valhyr.com/blogs/learn/the-norns

[7] https://vikingr.org/old-norse-texts/havamal#:~:text=I%20know%20that%20I%20hung,from%20what%20root%20it%20springs.

"given to Odin" is gefinn Óðni, a phrase that occurs many times throughout the Eddas and sagas in the context of human/ and animal sacrifices to Odin.[8]

---

[8] https://academic.oup.com/book/25964/chapter-abstract/193771177?redirectedFrom=fulltext

The Aetts of The Elder Futhark

What is an Aett? An Aett is a division amongst the Elder Futhark that contains eight runes. The Elder Futhark has 3 of these Aetts, (divisions), They are named Freyja's Aett, Hel's or Heimdall's Aett, and Tyr's Aett. These Aetts also take on a much deeper meaning than just a subsection of runes when you look at their groupings, and how the runes in each Aett correlate with one another.[9]

The Aetts are first seen in a set of jewelry dubbed the "Vadstena Bracteate," which depicts the three Aetts being separated by dots and was dated to the fifth century.[10] The Aetts to me and my praxis share a great deal with our concept of time, Wyrd (fate) and örlog (Past Actions). Wyrd is a Norse ideal closely associated with the idea of fate. It is the endpoint of all your actions as they are happening and have happened. Wyrd is not fixed and, ironically, it's not fatalistic. It can be changed, it can be worked with and have a different outcome. The way one's Wyrd is changed is through one's örlog.[11] Örlog is all your past actions up to now, which have created the Wyrd that you are experiencing right now. Your actions, or rather your örlog can change your Wyrd. We are on a path of expansion, growth, and knowledge when we take up the Runes. If we work with this path of growth, we create a Wyrd in which we should become something more than what we were. If we take up a path of non-expansion or no growth, we are working against our Wyrd and regressing to who we were before.

The Web of Wyrd is a neo-pagan or contemporary symbol, and is also referred to as Skuld's net and is seen by many, myself included, as the a representation of all of the cosmos's different Wyrds into one spider-like tapestry being woven by the Norns Urd, Verandi, and Skuld.[12]

---

[9] Chamberlain, Lisa. *Runes for Beginners: A Guide to Reading Runes in Divination, Rune Magic, and the Meaning of the Elder Futhark Runes*. Chamberlain Publications, 2018
[10] https://www.britannica.com/topic/Vadstena-Bracteate
[11] https://skaldskeep.com/norse/wyrd/
[12] https://berloga-workshop.com/blog/177-the-web-of-wyrd-the-matrix-of-fate-skulds-net.html

Web of Wyrd

The concept of Time/Wyrd/Örlog that is referred to with the runes and the Aetts is as follows: what is or was, what is becoming, and what should become, if you follow the path that you are on with actions you are taking. Each Aett lines up with each of the facets of this concept.

Freyja's Aett:
The first Aett belongs to Freya, Norse goddess whose many aspects include love, beauty, and fertility. This section of runes is all about love, happiness, and enjoyment, as well as physical presence and emotions. This Aett also speaks to beginnings, creation, and growth. In the first Aett, we are dealing with what we were in the past and what we are now. The Runes are related to what you have here in the present moment. They're presenting the tools you will need now. Each rune is a building block or footstep in progression, as if you're moving up a giant staircase. Here in these first few steps you are learning the lesson that you need to have now, and this information will build and become valuable throughout the path.

Heimdall's Aett:
In the next Aett, we are on the path of becoming something more than what we were. We are learning the lessons that we need to bring about this sense of becoming. Each Rune in this Aett is preparing you by teaching you lessons both harsh and needed in order to become the best version of you on this current path. We are getting in touch with an inner divinity we all have and it's still happening in the present, in the "Now" as we move from rune to rune in turn. Each rune in each Aett is building upon one another towards becoming our truest selves.

Tyr's Aett:
The last Aett is the path of what we should become if we have followed the path of runes up to now. If you have faced the shadows and the lessons and gone through each level of initiation that each rune represents, you are seeing the results of your work. You are reaping the benefits of taking the time to connect with these energies. This Aett is getting you closer in your relationship with your inner divinity and presents a path moving forward. You are reaping the rewards of the path that you have walked with the runes. You're achieving balances and solid foundational relationships with your higher self, and you now know what to do, having awakened to who you truly are.

Freya's Aett

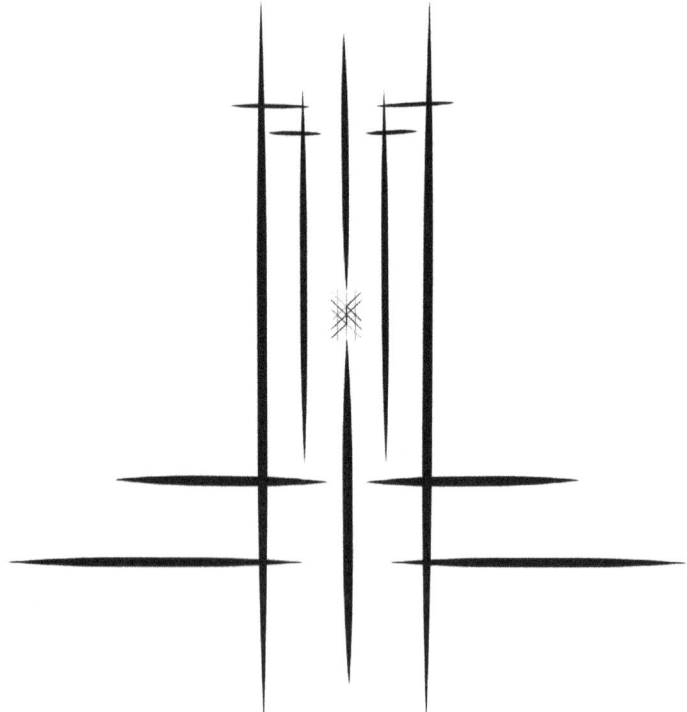

Fehu, Fé, Feoh

What is wealth measured?
It's something to give freely.
Let all be gracious.

Pronunciation: Fehu: FAY-hoo, Fé: fay, Feoh: Fay-Oh or foe
Literal Translation: Cattle, wealth, moveable property
Sounds: F, Fae, V
Magical Correspondences: Money magic, fertility, to bring positive change in favor of the querent, for comfort or healing. Reversed can do the opposite of the above uses with proper intent and actions.

Divination Meaning Upright:
All three rune's have a positive connotation. Drawing these rune's could mean that money or new possessions are coming into one's life. They could also indicate a positive change that's incoming, such as a special achievement, or awakening, or next step: something is coming to fruition. I consider Fehu a "YES" rune in most aspects. When in misery or grief, the drawing of any of these can bring comfort and acknowledgement that things are going to change in the way you wish.

Divination Meaning Upside Down:
If reversed, these runes serve as a warning against indulgence, teaching the lessons of greed or complacency, warning us to not sacrifice safety or the known in this particular instance. Take the time to think about what is to come, to weigh the risk and rewards.

Delving into the Runes:
As the beginning of each Futhark these runes very much symbolizes beginnings. The meaning of Fehu is reinforced by the rune's literal translation, "cattle," and the Norse myth of Auðhumla, who is the first ancestor of Uruz and the aurochs, the cow who was responsible for freeing the forefather of the Æsir from the ice in Ginnungagap.[13] Fé on the other hand represents the trade routes, and goods changing hands, stemming from Feoh and the wealth amassed in early England.

Fehu belongs to the goddess Freya, who presides over it both as a goddess of sensuality, beauty and abundance, but also as the mistress of magic. Fehu is intimately connected with the mysteries of hamingja, which is the force of luck and life possessed by living things. Fehu also

---
[13] https://www.britannica.com/topic/Audumla

has a strong correlation with the goddess Nerthus, the great Earth goddess. Cows were sacred to Nerthus, which serves as a reminder that all abundance comes from the Earth. All the foods we eat, every liquid we drink, all that we enjoy comes forth from the Earth, or Nerthus herself. She is a goddess of spring and prosperity to whom several Proto Germanic tribes paid tribute in hopes of a bountiful season.[14] The color that I most commonly associate with these three runes are varying shades of red and gold. It's interesting to note as well that red was almost universally the first color named across human cultures; it is also the color most easily created with natural dyes.[15] These three runes can represent the energy of life itself and are strongly associated with blood. When using any of these three in spellwork, be absolutely sure the kind of fertility you mean, or you may find that it is your "flocks and herds" that are increasing instead of your bank account. All three can be attributed to divine feminine presenting energy, as well as that of great healing. Many also find that Freyr particularly likes Fé.

It's worth noting that when studying the Younger Futhark it also brings to mind the sagas of old, and in Fé's case, the Saga of the Volsungs. The Norwegian Rune Poem contains an oblique reference to the Volsung Cycle. The second line, "the wolf is born and reared in the woods," echoes the story of the Volsungs when it refers to the life of a wolf in the woods. Both the Volsunga Saga and Fé tie into the meaning of dualistic wealth because as the saga and Norwegian Rune Poem both portray, the wolf is the most savage predator of the forests of old and could take cattle from farmers without recompense. Much akin to today's struggles in a capitalist society, make the wrong move fiscally and the wolves will be at your door to collect.

When it comes to Feoh it is of interest to note that among the four (F) Runes in the Futhorc, Feoh is the only one that is the phonetic equivalent of the Roman (F). It also can be used as a rune of self worth, reminding us to invest in what we wish to put out.

---

[14] https://www.britannica.com/topic/Germanic-religion-and-mythology

[15] https://nicolecicak.com/blog/2022/the-dark-twisted-history-of-color#:~:text=Red%20was%20the%20first%20pigment,used%20in%20prehistoric%20cave%20paintings.

Runic Notes

Fehu, Fé, Feoh

Date:
Time:
Lunar Phase:

What did the Rune(S) reveal to me?

How does this apply to me?

Runic Notes

Fehu, Fé, Feoh
Date:
Time:
Lunar Phase:

What did the Rune(S) reveal to me?

How does this apply to me?

Runic Notes
Fehu, Fé, Feoh
Date:
Time:
Lunar Phase:

What did the Rune(S) reveal to me?

How does this apply to me?

Uruz, Úr, Ur

Primal and Revered
Will be great strength and healing,
Untamed with courage

Pronunciation: Uruz: OO-rooz, Úr: Err, Ur: uur
Literal Translation: Aurochs a species of wild ox
Sound: U, Y, Ú, UR
Magical Correspondences: Strength, Willpower, Primal State, Healing, Change

Divination Meaning Upright:
The appearance of Uruz or the Futhorc's Ur in a reading upright says that the recipient of the reading will have all the strength necessary to do what's needed, but must be intelligent when going about it. The recipient must let go of ego and not subjugate others. It can also mean, in times of change, that it is time to commit and be courageous. If we take the Younger Futhark's Úr into account we see a change from primal energy to nature's prowess and the sudden danger or blessing that can come with severe weather.

Divination Meaning Reversed:
When seen reversed these runes are saying that you are in a period of challenges and opportunities, but you must be careful to not let your ambition and your. own personal power blind you, and lose out
on the objective, and maybe even burn important bridges.

Delving into the Runes:
Uruz of the Elder Futhark and Ur of the Futhorc are the runes of primal energy and strength. The Aurochs (the translation of Uruz) is the ancestor of the domestic cattle of the rune Fehu. Uruz is wild, untamed and full of potential. Uruz and Ur also represent health, endurance, and one of courage, while Úr represents cold rain and unnatural weather. Ur reminds us that we need to use aggression wisely so we do not flare out of control. All three runes contain the power of change, and although many do not like them because they are so primal or nature bound they are some of my favorites to use, as they help to channel the ancestral energy of those who went before, and help one to direct primal energy. Uruz and Ur are great for things that need an extra boost of strength, especially when it comes to new endeavors or creativity. But be wary when invoking or using Úr. Specifics matter; you could easily bring a disaster of a monsoon, instead of the cleansing of a mist.

While these runes' energies are heavily invested in the hamingja, they are not suited for easy, conscious control as Fehu is. They are all powerful unconscious shaping energies that need to be guided wisely as they manifest. They are an early reminder within the series that the untamed powers of creativity are not without danger – a reality quite clear in our modern technological civilization. It is the user's skill and practiced techniques that will control the energy unleashed by these runes. They are the runes of independence, of protecting one's territory.

The etymology of Uruz is unique when compared to the others as Uruz is *Ur* or *Yr* in Anglo-Saxon and *Ur* in Old Norse. It is akin to the "U" sound in English. Because Uruz is the aurochs, it is the symbol of wild, untamed power and uncontrolled potential. It means strength, wildness, masculinity, freedom, courage, and even change, often in a sudden and unexpected way. It can mean male sexuality, although that's usually reserved for Ingwaz.

It is also here that I wish to shed more light on the Younger's Úr and the connections it brings. Take the rain for example: here we look at the Grimnismal and kennings in Old Norse. In Griminsal 26 it is written that all of the waters of the world drip from the horns of the hart Eikthyrnir, who browses on the tree Laeradh that grows by Odin's Hall.[16] This can also be linked to the conjunction of the aurochs and where they lived: the wetlands. Going from the rain kenning mentioned we also see a related adjective úrigr(wet) which has a homonym meaning "ill tempered, and vicious," such as weather in non growing seasons. What we can glean from this and how it's discussed is that the kenning skára þverrir ("diminisher of mown fields") is Úr, where the wetlands invade the human enclaves through rain. Other weather related kennings worth mentioning here are hirðis hatr and versta veðr. Meaning "herdsman hatred, and worst weather" respectively, both these kennings of Úr came from the predation of animals on livestock and how they primarily took place at night, during fog or heavy rain.

The Norwegian Rune Poem found in the book "Long Branches of the Younger Futhark" has the following lines and its here we find a notable change from aurochs to slag: Úr er af illu jarne; opt løypr ræinn á hjarne- Slag is from bad iron; the reindeer often bounds over the frozen snow.[17] It's easy to understand the message behind the second line of the poem: when faced with adversity one must overcome it. How we dig out this third rather confusing meaning is the question; for that we turn to the phrase Það ýrir í "(something) it glitters like drops of dew."According to scholars Cleasby and Vigfusson, this phrase was also applied to the glittering particles of slag in iron ore. In the process of extracting the ore it's said that the fewer particles it has, the better the iron is. This process produced a proverb that blames granulated iron for a soft knife.

It is the culmination of the three etymological meanings of Úr that brings us full circle: wild beasts, cold hard rain, and melting slag all paint a picture of the cosmology of the Norse creation myth, of Aduhmbla, of the chasm known as the Ginnungagap. With all three

---

[16] https://www.voluspa.org/grimnismal.htm
[17] pg. 41-51 of afformentioned book

meanings, we are reminded of the dangers and pitfalls that come with great primal forces: will they be blessings, or destruction?

Runic Notes
Uruz, Úr, Ur
Date:
Time:
Lunar Phase:

What did the Rune(S) reveal to me?

How does this apply to me?

Runic Notes
Uruz, Úr, Ur
Date:
Time:
Lunar Phase:

What did the Rune(S) reveal to me?

How does this apply to me?

Runic Notes
Uruz, Úr, Ur
Date:
Time:
Lunar Phase:

What did the Rune(S) reveal to me?

How does this apply to me?

Thurisaz, Thurs, ᚦorn

A thorn or thunder,
Always there unrelenting.
Nature bides its time.

Pronunciation: Thurisaz: THOR-ee-sahz, Thurs: thoours, ᚦorn: th-oo-rrn
Literal Translation: giant, thorn, Thor,
Sound: TH
Magical Correspondences: Invoking Thor, invoking weather, Power, action, protection or defense.

Divination Meaning Upright:
The three ᚦ runes although similar in meaning can vary widely, and it's here that in divination you'll see the most impact. The Younger's Thurs is a Rune of action, of brute force. The Rune Thurs is the iconic action of Thor swinging Mjolnir; and as such when appearing in a reading it should carry such weight impacting the context greatly. Thurisaz on the other hand is reminiscent of the thunder god's lightning, reminding us that before he was Thor he was Donar, as unpredictable as nature.[18] We see this in readings as a call for protection: either to seek it, or to give it, or as a confirmation that Thor is present. Then we have ᚦorn, the Futhorc's rune of the literal thorn, harkening to the imagery of a hawthorn bush. Just as the bush itself is a warning to leave it alone so is ᚦorn when appearing in a reading.

Divination Meaning if Reversed:
In the case of Thurisaz and Thurs, you need to check yourself and do some serious thinking before you react or act upon impulse. Take a big step back, breathe and pause. In the case of ᚦorn reversed, it's essentially the positive connotation indicated saying this is your green light.

Delving into the Rune:
It's not uncommon for the rune meaning of Thurisaz to have kinship with ᚦorn, often being described as a thorn that is most sharp, a grim and evil thing to take grip on or touch. However, both Thurisaz and Thurs are in some way representative of Thor (Thurisaz,) and his hammer being swung (Thurs). Protecting Asgard from the giants who resist the expansion of consciousness throughout the multiverse. In every respect, the energies of Thurisaz are a forceful enemy of unconsciousness, ignorance and the rule of brute violence. Thurisaz represents the warrior that combines consciousness and wisdom with matters requiring force;

---

[18] https://youtu.be/v403HBVzV9I?si=epn6fXczMjTv2Zml

it's here that Thurs blends its identity with Thurisaz as representation of Mjolnir hitting its target.

Thurisaz is a rune of fertility in the sense that it destroys arid and hard, rocky ground and turns it into a workable soil that bears fruit and crops by means of rain and storms. The best state of mind for working with the rune is enthusiasm, rather than anger or fear, as the former will support the right awareness much better and lessen the potential danger of facing the mighty Thurisaz magic.

Þorn is a warning when it appears in a divination. It is saying, "Don't touch!" There may be a temptation to gather haws or to rest in the shade, but to do so is to risk pain. The querent may choose to move forward anyway – to enter the hawthorn grove – but he should proceed with caution. Keep in mind always that thorn represents a potential hazard, and not an unavoidable hazard.

Runic Notes
Thurisaz, Thurs, ᚦorn
Date:
Time:
Lunar Phase:

What did the Rune(S) reveal to me?

How does this apply to me?

Runic Notes
Thurisaz, Thurs, ᚦorn
Date:
Time:
Lunar Phase:

What did the Rune(S) reveal to me?

How does this apply to me?

Runic Notes
Thurisaz, Thurs, Þorn
<u>Date:</u>
<u>Time:</u>
<u>Lunar Phase:</u>

What did the Rune(S) reveal to me?

How does this apply to me?

Ansuz, As, Os

ᚨ, ᚫ, ᚮ

Poems, Prose, or Meter
Through mouth or Pen, wisdoms sought.
Paths not as they seem.

Pronunciation: Ansuz: AHN-sooz, As: OOs, Os: ahhs
Literal Translation: A God, Mouth
Sound: A, AN, Oh, Q, Os, O
Magical Correspondences: Help with speech or poetry, help speed up communication, knowledge, pattern recognition or code breaking

Divination Meaning Upright:
Ansuz, As, and Os: Speech, order, and breath. When any of these runes appear it reveals to us that the answers are found in ourselves. It is time to do some self care, speak those affirmations and take a breath. As appearing in a reading is a signal to stop: to pay attention to what is happening, and interpret the signals around you, and hear what they say. Meanwhile, Ansuz recommends illuminating one's confusion by seeking information and expanding one's knowledge. Many times, we get stuck just because we don't know that there are other possibilities, other paths to take, and this is when Os appears, reminding us that our path is innate, and to take a breath. All three runes encourage us to discover the seemingly hidden ways: both those inside us and the ones revealed in our surroundings.

Divination Meaning Reversed:
Many Runes have complex reversed meanings that can make the guidance take a different direction. Not these three: when any of these come up reversed, it's a full stop and throw the brakes moment. Whether it's a writing block or a failure to speak, these three runes will tell you exactly why. Look to the rune(s) that are cast or pulled after them, and those runes will be the reason to make the full stop and reevaluate.

Delving into the Runes:
Ansuz, As, and Os make for one of the more powerful and scintillating combinations of Runes across the systems. For me, they combine Bragi's words, Loki's tongue, and Odin's wisdom into one world shattering package. It's important to note that all three Runes are the first Runes of the runic systems that correspond with Odin, who set the standard for self sacrifice to discover the runes.

Os in my opinion has the strongest correlation, being the rune of breath. In the myth cycle, Odin breathed life into Ask and Embla, the first man and woman, born from two logs (Ask of ash, Embla of elm).[19] The root energy of Os triggers inspiration and ecstatic mental states.

Then we have As, the Rune of divine order, symbolic of our mind's ability to work with patterns. A sense of governance is innate in As, and it will seek to put things into proper boxes of organization. As governs our mental capacities to name all things. Whereas Thurisaz deals with chaotic forces, As is a rune of order.

Ansuz is the rune of poetry, of the skalds and bards, and in my opinion shares correspondences with Bragi, the god of poetry, associated with the throat energy center,, spellwork, and incantations, and in part is quite significant in the ritual of naming. Naming a thing properly can give power over that thing, and in ancient traditions, naming has often been used to dispel mischievous spirits, bind malevolent forces, or break psychological fetters. The relationship also indicates that chaotic events can be used to shape ordered circumstances and one's own thoughts, or the thoughts of others. Ansuz is suggestive of the relentless patterns that modern chaos theory declares are universal in every system. The newest theories of language are also found in the mysterious order and 'strange attractors' of chaos linguistics.[20]

Any of these three Runes will tell you to pay close attention to what the gods are telling you. They involve a sort of wake-up call that may be reaching out through a song, book, poem or the words of kin, asking you to either spring into action or wait, depending on the other Runes in the cast. Sometimes they're an unwelcome guest because they don't sugar coat things. They will say what you need to hear without taking your emotions into account. Pay attention to the messages when Ansuz, As, or Os appear. The gods are listening and have given you direction.

---

[19] https://www.britannica.com/topic/Askr-and-Embla

[20] https://medium.com/age-of-awareness/8-ways-chaos-theory-explains-how-we-learn-new-languages-af61889eac40

Runic Notes
Ansuz, As, Os
Date:
Time:
Lunar Phase:

What did the Rune(S) reveal to me?

How does this apply to me?

Runic Notes
Ansuz, As, Os
Date:
Time:
Lunar Phase:

What did the Rune(S) reveal to me?

How does this apply to me?

Runic Notes
Ansuz, As, Os
Date:
Time:
Lunar Phase:

What did the Rune(S) reveal to me?

How does this apply to me?

Raidho, Reið, Rad

Heimdall, I call thee.
Protection, and clear pathways
Far beyond the Nine.

Pronunciation: Raidho: Ride-hoe, Reið: wraith, Rad: raad
Literal Translation: Journey, riding, wheel.
Sound: R
Magical Correspondences: Travel, Clear routes, healing or help, protection, cycles

Divination Meaning Upright:
Associated with communication and the ultimate harmony of the elements at the end of a long journey, these three runes share a cumulative meaning. The person being cast or read for is enduring some struggle, trauma, or adversity that they are trying to resolve. When any of the three appear they are giving the message of keeping the faith in the fact that the problem that torments us will soon be definitively solved, as long as we keep our goals clear and are persevering. Raidho, Reið, and Rad all share the same base meaning of the journey: whether spiritual or physical, trust in the process.

Divination Meaning Reversed:
We should look inward. It is very likely that we have not reached the goals we set ourselves because our mental attitude is negative, such as not believing in our projects, nor in our abilities because we are acting in the wrong way. We must stop justifying ourselves and not accepting reality, but rather face the facts and make the necessary decisions, even if they are unpleasant. Only in this way can we go further. These runes remind us that we must go forward, step by step, without fear of facing adversity.

Delving into the Runes:
Raidho, Reið, and Rad all revolve around horses, riding, and journeys. They are the first occurrence in the runic systems where their base meanings all stay the same. Raidho in particular is most seen in congruence with transportation and is well suited to use for journeys and road travel. Just like the rhythms and sounds of the wheels of vehicles and hooves of the horses, Raidho pertains to cycles and rhythms. Similarly, Reið refers to how one must turn the wheel back to right itself. Rad on the other hand, will urge you to control yourself and your ego. No matter how far or how comfortable you are in your journey, there is always an air of uncertainty and unknown danger when traveling (both spiritually and physically). These three runes help ensure that you and your cargo of both kinds arrive safely.

Raidho, Reið, and Rad are runes of leading by example, and that actions speak louder than words. Though Ansuz may tell the stories, Raidho, Reið, and Rad live the stories. They represent our deepest personal life journey, and the ultimate failures of language to communicate our experience to others. Something to notice about them is the habitual way in which our minds concoct story and identity in more than one facet of our lives striving to always journey into the depths of who we are and how to be our most genuine selves.

Use Rad to recognize the direction in which your daily life pulls you, for there is a compass within you that can be accessed using the energy of this rune, following your interests and your loves your greatest wishes and your dreams. Then Raidho will step in as the compass to navigate that inner world. By meditating on Reið you will begin to see time and space as a personal reality, rather than something imposed on you from outside. All three pieces represent the same journey from slightly different angles.

The symbols that can be connected to these runes are the cosmic tree Yggdrasil, and Odin upon his horse Sleipnir, which in tandem symbolize the profound understanding of the meaning of life that can only be obtained by traveling through the nine worlds. This pairing also indicates the strength and energy needed when we decide to embark on a journey. The third connected symbol is Heimdall, the watcher and first guardian of the realms, seeing all possibilities, the twist and turns of eons, just as we seek to use these runes to navigate ourselves.

Runic Notes
Raidho, Reið, Rad
Date:
Time:
Lunar Phase:

What did the Rune(S) reveal to me?

How does this apply to me?

Runic Notes
Raidho, Reið, Rad
Date:
Time:
Lunar Phase:

What did the Rune(S) reveal to me?

How does this apply to me?

Runic Notes
Raidho, Reið, Rad
Date:
Time:
Lunar Phase:

What did the Rune(S) reveal to me?

How does this apply to me?

Kenaz, Kaun, Cen

⟨ , ᚲ , ᚴ

Inspiring through flame,
Creations find their shape.
Be wary of heat

Pronunciation: Kenaz: KAY-nahz, Kaun: CAWn, Cen: Ken
Literal Translation: Torch, Ulcer, Knowing
Sound: C, K, CK, G
Magical Correspondences: Passion, fire, creation, lust, change, insight, illumination, renewal

Divination Meaning Upright:
When Kenaz is cast or pulled, it signifies that you are in a moment when you are forced to make a decision. Kenaz invites you to gather the strength and wisdom needed to accept your own transformations and positive changes. It advises us to free ourselves from the old prejudices that we disguise with excuses that we are used to using ("I am like that," "I cannot change," or "I cannot act differently"), and to accept the opportunities that life offers, to take advantage of them. Kenaz supports open and wise attitudes, and rejects dullness and closed-mindedness. When Kaun appears it's time for some transformation through trials. Although Kaun stands for a wound, we must understand that it is through the suffering of such a wound that we gain new insight (think back to Odin's ordeal). This rune is symbolic of just that, the new insight that we gain from a wound and the healing that comes from it. Then we have Cen: the bridge between the two, being both a beacon and the touch that caused wounding. When Cen appears alongside Rad, Raidho or Reið it serves as the catalyst for a truly eye-opening spiritual awakening. Due to this bridge symbology, Cen is also a reminder of our inner fire, and how it can burn as an infection trying to heal and clear the chaff away so we may grow in ourselves.

Divination Meaning Reversed:
When any of these three runes is read reversed, it is announcing the end of something. Whether you will experience a loss of a relationship, of an endeavor, or another important aspect of your life, will depend on the runes around it. These outcomes are always difficult to face and overcome, but these Runes advise you to accept reality, and learn from it. Maintain a constructive attitude and learn from your experiences. No matter the circumstance, the crisis that comes, be it at the end of a friendship, the end of a romantic relationship, or a change in the professional field, will lead to personal growth.

Delving into the Runes:
Kenaz is Loki's rune, the rune of fire, change and inspiration. Kenaz is a reminder that the energy of truth and knowledge may harm us, and is literally translated as torch. Meanwhile Kaun is translated as a disease or ulcer. These two meanings tie into the dichotomy of how wisdom affects us, and we are no longer able to wallow in the "ignorance is bliss" paradigm. Once you know, you can't "unknow," and that is where we find the bridge: Cen. Another phrase that suits these three runes is that sometimes the truth hurts. But with all that seemingly negative connotation, Kenaz, Kaun, and Cen all can indicate and herald a moment of enlightenment, illumination and light. When carrying these runes you are driving back the unknown, and driving back ignorance. Then, after uncovering your lesson, you're called to teach, and to continue passing the knowledge (the torch) along. The fire of inspiration and creativity to which Kenaz refers is very much the same as that which Brokk and Eitri, two of the greatest dwarven Smiths, used to make some of the Æsir's greatest treasures and tools, including Mjölnir.

Cen in a similar context means availability and creativity. Choosing and/or making decisions isn't always easy. Cen advises us to let ourselves be guided by our inner light of reason and knowledge. Only in this way, when we have to choose between passion and love, between truth and deception, will we be able to distinguish the right way without confusing our goals with desires that sometimes blind the will.

With all three, we renew ourselves, we abandon old habits and old vices: every obstacle for us becomes a challenge to grow and learn something new, both of personal conscience and of collective existence. They are the fire of transformation, the alchemical element par excellence, presiding over all the processes of raw and dark matter to make it clear and luminous. The amount of energy around us is immense, enclosed in even the smallest object, and the fire of this rune helps us to release the energy trapped in the matter, transforming it. Enlightenment needs to be tempered with wisdom before its true worth and power can be known.

Runic Notes
Kenaz, Kaun, Cen
Date:
Time:
Lunar Phase:

What did the Rune(S) reveal to me?

How does this apply to me?

Runic Notes
Kenaz, Kaun, Cen
Date:
Time:
Lunar Phase:

What did the Rune(S) reveal to me?

How does this apply to me?

Runic Notes
Kenaz, Kaun, Cen
Date:
Time:
Lunar Phase:

What did the Rune(S) reveal to me?

How does this apply to me?

Gebo, - , Gifu

Gifts plenty bestowed,
To share with all, who claim kin.
With this, reap honor

Pronunciation: Gebo: GHEB-o, Gifu: Gee-foo
Literal Translation: Gift
Sound: G
Magical Correspondences: balance, neutrality, gifts, numerology of seven, wealth or finances to be shared

Divination Meaning Upright:

Gebo and Gifu do not possess the ability to be cast or pulled upside down. This characteristic symbolizes the greatest gift that has been given to all beings: freedom, from which all that is beautiful in life derives. Gebo's message, upright or upside down, will always be the same: the beauty that is in the reciprocity of actions, whether it be services, energy or other means. The gift that Gifu yields is that of sacrifice. Gifu takes the giving a step further than appreciation and generosity, and makes it a point to show that this gift is so important that they involved the gods to do so.

However, the cross of Gebo and Gifu, the archetypal symbol of suffering, reminds us that you can only receive it if you have given it. Only if you are generous can you be repaid. We must learn to accept the gifts with which we are welcomed by nature (divine or earthly) and the people around us, but we must also get used to putting our virtues to good use in favor of others. It is here that we see Gifu's wisdom come forth, signifying the transition between the two.

Both runes remind us that we are independent and free beings, and that in any relationship (professional, sentimental, or friendship), we are happy only if we know how to maintain our independence. It also warns you, however, that you must not settle or cancel yourself in this union.

There is no "standard" reverse interpretation, but as you progress in your path you may find that it shows you a reversal of imagery. Allow the context of the reading and the revelations of the runes to lead the way.

Delving Into the Runes:
Here we see how the Runic systems begin to change. Gebo is the first of eight runes to be dissolved into the other runes and sounds of the Younger Futhark. This leaves Gebo from the Elder Futhark, the rune of repricoicity, gifts, and balance, and its Runic system counterpart Gifu -from the Futhorc, the rune of gifts and blessings from sacrifice and the gods. Both Gebo and Gifu are also the seventh runes in the Runic Systems which brings to mind the powerful numerology of lucky number seven. Both are runes of gifts: not necessarily material, but definitely ancestral and spiritual. The Ancient Norse were extremely practical people who believed hospitality and equal exchange to be of the highest priority.[21] As we saw with Fehu, Fé, and Feoh, when one brings forward wealth it is important to distribute it equally in a balanced manner so all can flourish. Gifu rules over esoteric exchange, and this is seen in the offerings of then and now: if you ask the gods for help and they make it so the universe provides, whether directly or indirectly, it's only fair we say thank you and give a gift in return.

Gebo, however, doesn't necessarily mean that the gift comes with strings attached. If they are, the strings may be of the expected variety, such as a birthday present, a holiday present, or some other giving time, like a wedding shower or baby shower. Sometimes the gift does have strings attached, but it's up to you to determine if the gift is an opportunity you wish to take advantage of. Gebo can mean a gift from the gods, but it also suggests a partnership between you and the god or goddess who is offering the gift.

The meaning of both Gebo and Gifu can depend on the runes surrounding them. The runes feed off of each other, creating a broader picture for the caster. These runes almost always allude to gifts and/or partnerships, but the other runes around them may dictate how that gift or partnership fits in context with everything else.

---

[21] https://www.visitnorway.com/things-to-do/art-culture/vikings/

Runic Notes

Gebo, Gifu
Date:
Time:
Lunar Phase:

What did the Rune(S) reveal to me?

How does this apply to me?

Runic Notes
Gebo, Gifu
Date:
Time:
Lunar Phase:

What did the Rune(S) reveal to me?

How does this apply to me?

Wunjo, - , Wyn

With joy there is pain,
Balance inwards to bring peace.
Cry, and you shall smile.

Pronunciation: Wunjo: WOON-yo, Wyn: When
Literal Translation: Joy Bliss, Peace
Sound: W, U
Magical Correspondences: Joy, happiness, family, harmony, peace

Divination Meaning Upright:
When Wunjo comes out upright, it indicates that you are experiencing a favorable moment, as you feel in harmony with life and at peace. It is an ideal attitude to accept changes, to gain confidence in yourself and in what you are doing. For this reason, Wunjo suggests a "rebirth," the beginning of a regenerative path, which does not necessarily have to translate into a physical change (of work, residence, or other). Wunjo suggests seeking harmony between the different aspects of life, and in all likelihood, this adjustment will enhance one's current well-being, and make it last.

Divination Meaning Reversed:
If Wunjo comes out upside down, it means that it is necessary to free oneself from all the negative experiences of the past (deceptions, resentments, and guilt, among others) that do not allow us to be happily fulfilled in the present. The time has come to strip off the old and embrace the novelties that life presents. Wunjo reversed recommends meditating to achieve a calmer state of mind. Patience and perseverance will be fundamental in this moment of crisis. Everything happens at the right time; therefore, many problems will be avoided if you can control your impatience.

Delving into the Runes:
Wunjo and Wyn finish up the first aett of the Elder Futhark, and the first eight of the Anglo-Saxon Futhorc. As we can see with the first eight runes of the Elder Futhark, those belonging to Freya's Aett, we have been on a journey of strength and abundance, of giving and sharing. Wunjo is the eighth rune of the Elder Futhark and is the rune of joy and bliss. It shows us what comes about when living by the principles of the seven runes that preceded it. Wyn takes this joy to a different level, and hints towards the ecstatic bliss that comes with intimate and carnal desires. -In a reading we see that as passion and wanting: a thirst for the outcome of the query asked.

The Wunjo rune means light and happiness. A bearer of good news, synonymous with luck and gladness after an adverse period as well as convalescence and self-confidence. It is the reward for sacrifices made: the prospects for the future look bright. Wunjo symbolizes the link between the most diverse opinions that blend harmoniously, culminating in friendship and goodwill. This rune also indicates the sense of familial pride. It is known as the rune of the happiness of victory.

Wyn can be sometimes associated with the god Odin (or Woden, in the Futhorc's age). It appears to finally announce success after the efforts made to achieve a goal. When these runes appear, they herald the feeling of pleasure and release and the great feeling of peace that we experience when we live in balance with ourselves and with nature. From the union of destinies, lives, and energies in Gebo, something wonderful and unique is born: Wunjo, the inner child, the innocent, the spirit, the essence, the love that takes shape from the union of the masculine and of the feminine.

Runic Notes
Wunjo, Wyn
Date:
Time:
Lunar Phase:

What did the Rune(S) reveal to me?

How does this apply to me?

Runic Notes
Wunjo, Wyn
Date:
Time:
Lunar Phase:

What did the Rune(S) reveal to me?

How does this apply to me?

Heimdall's Aett

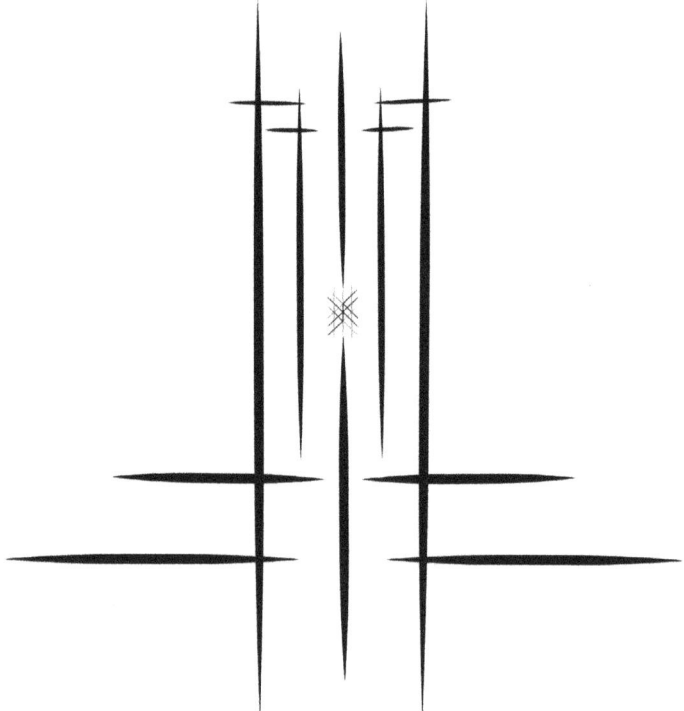

Hagalaz, Hagall, Hegel

First of the Mystics
Urd, bringing growth from release.
The Well finds one's past

Pronunciation: Hagalaz: HA-ga-lahz, Hagall: HA-Gaul, Hegel: heh-gill
Literal Translation: Hail
Sound: H
Magical Correspondences: bridges broke, abrupt change, liberation, bravery, invoking Hel Urd, or Heimdall, destiny, optimism

Divination Meaning Upright:
The extraction of these runes in a cast or pull indicate that liberation from the stagnancy of patterns that we are complacent in is imminent. I use extraction because we as a society fear and loathe change, and these runes bring just that. It is necessary to ask ourselves about the relationship we have with the varying types of endings we experience, including death. We have to be able to answer whether we can accept these endings. Can we face them with a serene mind, and can we accept the inevitability of destiny? Hagalaz can indicate a problem of rigidity, of captivity due to patterns, rules, and morals. It is a rune that allows access to new levels of knowledge through the joint work of destruction and creation, of death and rebirth.

All three runes sing of destiny, and how we look to the past to motivate our future endeavors to create a legacy. But in doing so, in the true fashion of the destruction that hail can bring, they also imply liberation from the past and acceptance of decisions once made. The advice given is to let yourself be guided, and be in tune with your nature. In the case of love, you might go through a difficult time, afraid of not reaching happiness, with doubts and uncertainties, and worries that you could make mistakes. Be patient and stay calm, don't face difficult situations yet, and wait for the moment to pass. At work, many sacrifices may be required; it can be hard, even unbearable, and there could be a risk of losing your job. Grit your teeth and move forward without losing sight of your goals. It matters of health, there is a risk of getting sick; you need to dedicate more time to yourself and to your hobbies, to relax and recover lost energy. It happens sometimes that, despite all the precautions taken, fate chooses for us by breaking up a relationship of love or friendship, depriving us of a steady job or a person dear to us. We must remember that life goes on despite everything, that all of this around us is a spinning wheel. There will be other loves, other people ready to have us next to them, other jobs, new satisfactions, other people to know, children and grandchildren who are born with a new promise and a new hope. Change is inevitable and we must be able to accept it.

Divination Meaning Reversed:
Reversed, these runes with the exception of Hagall mean that the coming change is already here, and it is not going to manifest in a healthy or positive way. Essentially, it is too late to change, and there will be a negative outcome. Nature rules the runes of hail; these are runes that represent the immutable forces that we must accept. They announce dysfunction, and destruction in multiple forms. All three runes can carry negative connotations in this position.

Delving into the Runes:
Hagalaz is Hel's rune, and also the first of the Norns' runes. Hagalaz relates to Urd. Urd, Verandi, and Skuld (that which is, becoming, and debt) are the three Norns who tend to Urd's well at the base of Yggdrasil, watering the roots of the great world tree while seeing and watching the Web of Wyrd take its shape, carving the names of the many into stone. Hagalaz, Hagall, and Hegel are the forces of nature under which many suffer: ice, the cold, and the hail. But there is a reminder to stay optimistic: No hailstorm can last forever, and the sun always returns. When the sun does indeed return, it will melt the hail that is on the ground, and any crops that remain standing will be nourished by the resulting water.

Yes, there is a disruption around you, a force of nature over your head with which you must contend, but Hegel reminds you to be strong and to wait for the sun to return. You can see how this melting of ice and the flow of water helps remove blockages, from rivers that thaw in the spring and rush toward the ocean to the tears that spring forth as you let emotions flow from you.

These three runes remind us to remain steadfast in the face of adversity, and it is this perseverance that helps us succeed. Each of our ancestors were people who suffered adversity without which you wouldn't be here today. The interpretation of these runes refers to the moment you are living in: perhaps it is happy because life as a couple is about to begin, or perhaps it is painful due to the loss of someone you love or because you are going through a moment of crisis. The details of Hagalaz, Hagall, and Hegel will also depend on the message of the other runes in a reading or cast.

Runic Notes
Hagalaz, Hagall, Hegel
Date:
Time:
Lunar Phase:

What did the Rune(S) reveal to me?

How does this apply to me?

Runic Notes
Hagalaz, Hagall, Hegel
Date:
Time:
Lunar Phase:

What did the Rune(S) reveal to me?

How does this apply to me?

Runic Notes
Hagalaz, Hagall, Hegel
Date:
Time:
Lunar Phase:

What did the Rune(S) reveal to me?

How does this apply to me?

Nauthiz, Nauðr, Nyd

ᚾ

Duty to oneself
Paramount it is to heal
Present and Lucid

Pronunciation: Nauthiz: NAW-theez, Nauðr: Nae-thher, Nyd: Need
Literal Translation: need, duty, restraint. plight, need-fire, constraint
Sound: N
Magical Correspondences: Necessity, self care, reality, invoking Verandi, burdens, harsh lessons

Divination Meaning Upright:
What you want doesn't always coincide with what you really need, and this makes you dissatisfied. It is likely that you are at a time when you are dominated by nostalgia and expectations. Nauthiz, Nauðr, and Nyd recommend a rest period to focus on what you actually "need." Here is where many place an emphasis on the idea of balance, and while balance is a necessity, it is not achievable with a single one step. When these runes arrive in a reading, they are saying to take the first steps needed towards that balance. These runes will allow you to place yourself in the present, which is the only physical reality we can change, to accept it and to learn from it. These runes signal that if you spend your time fantasizing about the future or regretting the past, you will lose the best part of your life: the present. Its advice is to be lucid and live in a coherent way with yourself and your possibilities. Some hopes have been frustrated, or perhaps you have expectations that are not achievable.

Divination Meaning Reversed:
Reversed, Nauthiz, Nauðr, and Nyd are great teachers disguised as messengers of afflictions and limitations. It is said that only by reaching the peak of darkness, can we begin to become aware of the light that radiates from our unconscious, our need-fire. When something that is part of our interior is denied, that which has been so "rejected" causes destruction. Here it becomes necessary to purify yourself: by setting out to do this, you will consolidate your will and strength of character. Start with the hardest issues and work your way up to the easier things. Or, on the contrary, start with the simpler ones and continue with the more difficult ones. Remember that the term "suffer" originally meant only "endure." You may therefore be required to endure the dark moments of your journey, calling them to light, controlling anger, suppressing impulses, and keeping yourself intact, both spiritually and physically. That is what's at stake. Modesty, availability, and honesty are absolutely crucial in these situations.

Delving into the Runes:

Nauthiz is the second rune of the Norns in the Elder Futhark, belonging to Verandi (that which is currently happening). Nauthiz is another rune that doesn't have many rosy or cheery connotations. As with Hagalaz and Isa, and their other Runic system counterparts, Nauthiz, Nauðr, and Nyd speak of frustration and hardship. The appearance of these three runes in a reading means that you are most likely constrained, or about to be, by an unavoidable situation or person. This means you'll find yourself, if you haven't already, in a place where it's difficult to maneuver or find some semblance of peace. Suffering is an inherent part of these runes. Nauthiz, Nauðr, and Nyd mean need, repression, and pain. They represent the maturation of ideas and intentions or, in the case of birth, expectation and destiny, which bears fruit as long as you have patience.

They are the metaphor of the ones who carry an uncomfortable and heavy burden. They also evoke a sense of endurance, and give the strength to accept suffering willingly, making it as productive as possible, even if the hope that better times will come is very low. Many times, we want to achieve a goal (to be strong, or to find our way in life), and yet have the wrong concept of how to achieve this goal. These three runes recommend experiencing weakness to learn what it means to be strong, or "getting lost" to find out what the real path is. They advise you to clarify your ideas and define your desires. Without resistance, form would fall apart. Every action has an equal and opposite reaction. They represent the basic resistance of unconscious forces against newly evolved consciousness, but also the overwhelming need for evolution of consciousness, and that unconscious resistance to it.

The mysteries of necessity are at the core of Nauthiz, Nauðr, and Nyd. They are central to manipulating our own Wyrd, so that desired outcomes can be attained through navigating the energies of the Norns. Invoking need is more powerful than wishing, but what we need and what we desire are not always the same. In this sense, Nauthiz, Nauðr, and Nyd can protect us from ourselves, but their lessons are often harsh.

Runic Notes
Nauthiz, Nauðr, Nyd
Date:
Time:
Lunar Phase:

What did the Rune(S) reveal to me?

How does this apply to me?

Runic Notes
Nauthiz, Nauðr, Nyd
Date:
Time:
Lunar Phase:

What did the Rune(S) reveal to me?

How does this apply to me?

Runic Notes
Nauthiz, Nauðr, Nyd
Date:
Time:
Lunar Phase:

What did the Rune(S) reveal to me?

How does this apply to me?

Isa, Ísa, Is

|

Glacial in approach
What will the Ice reveal now?
Patience proves fruitful.

Pronunciation: Isa: EE-sa. Ísa: eye-sa, Is: eese
Literal Translation: Ice
Sound: I, EE, J. E, É, Í
Magical Correspondences: Ice, patience, order, scrying, mirror, danger, warning, trust, secrets, invoking Skuld

Divination Meaning Upright:
These runes can be deceiving in spite of their silent and imperceptible nature. They can paralyze the raging waves beneath the surface and erect static monuments with water from waterfalls and springs, as proof of their strength. Ice subtly prevents action. It would be prudent to freeze matters involving the consultant until the "thaw," which removes the isolation when everything starts up again with renewed enthusiasm.

Known as the runes of stasis and order, Isa, Ísa, and Is want to show us that there is no place for distrust in ourselves as long as we have breath. Everything has its time, its moment. It may be that apparently nothing is happening to us, but instead, we are unconsciously evaluating our past, an indispensable phase in order to face the future. When this rune appears, depending on the context of the reading it is very likely that you are in a kind of lethargy. Something is developing within you, perhaps a creative idea, a project, a change of work or, simply, you need time to think, to review the present and the past, and to look towards the future without, for the moment, anything intervening. It can be useful, at times, to stop acting and to bring order to one's inner world. We must not force things.

Isa, Ísa, and Is recommends having patience. This is a time of contemplation and meditation, not of sadness; there's no need to feel guilty about your inertia. You must always remember that after the hibernation of winter comes the explosion of life in spring. Isa assures you that after this period of calm, your potential will be greater, as you will have had time to get to know yourself better and understand your feelings.

There is no "standard" reverse interpretation, but as you progress in your path you may find that it shows you a reversal of imagery or negative language. Allow the context of the reading and the revelations of the runes lead the way.

Delving into the Runes:
Isa is the rune of the third and final Norn, Skuld the future (that which should become), in the Elder Futhark. As we have learned through Hagalaz, the ancient Norse knew the inherent dangers of ice. That is what Isa, Ísa, and Is represent: ice itself. These runes are the ice that is all around us, springing forth from the Earth. As we look upon the mighty strength of glaciers and icebergs, we can see how ice could almost be considered an element itself, water brought to bear in a most mighty form.

Ice is dangerous. For those of us who live closer to poles, we deal with the potential for ice for much of the year. Ice can be treacherous to walk upon, and we must always be cautious when walking on an icy surface, whether it's ice on the ground or ice on a pond. Ice slows and eventually stops the movement of water, and as such these runes are the energy of stasis, and of stillness. When these three runes appear in a cast or reading, something in your life is frozen. Isa, Ísa, and Is symbolize tiredness, renunciation, and withdrawal. Like the previous runes related to death and pain, these are associated with emptiness, silence, mourning, and those states of consciousness that accompany and surround death, whose pain is not excruciating but becomes sadness, melancholy, and loss of sense.

The thought of death can evoke fear, bewilderment, and helplessness. Isa, Ísa, and Is help us to grasp the importance of the present moment, of what is here and now, and invite us to divert attention from what is no longer there. If you remain tied to the past, something in you dies along with that which has died. You cannot live in mourning for your whole life; Isa, Ísa, and Is are used to cry all the tears you have, overcome the pain, and come back to life again. They help us to accept inevitable separation, to dissolve the bonds of our soul from the illusion that those pieces of us now gone are still needed. Some do not resign themselves to the loss and change that comes with grieving and continue to live as if they were dead instead: they are dull, they have renounced rebirth, and they live a slow agony made up of regrets, complaints, and feelings of guilt. Isa, Ísa, and Is are the ice, the winter, the apparent end of everything. But under the ice of winter, life pulsates, seeds sprout, and spring is preparing, getting ready to cover the earth with green, starting a new cycle.

These three runes teach us that death does not exist as we think of it, but that it is rather a part of life: it is a fundamental, essential aspect, a transitory state that characterizes being. Everything that exists in nature has a beginning and an end, but also a new rebirth, often in another form. Ice is like a veil that covers the earth: it is very bright, dazzling, but also deceptive; it is the veil of time, the veil of illusion that does not let you see what it really is. Isa, Ísa, and Is help us recognize this illusion, along with what is making things appear different from how they are. Do not fall too hastily, though, for what they present as truth, for sometimes ice is the illusion. Just as ice that is destined to melt under the rays of the sun reveals that which is beneath, so too can our consciousness through illumination reveal a hidden reality.

Isa, Ísa, and Is are often associated with the Norse goddess Hel, Queen of the kingdom of Helheim. Her realm is often placed next to one of the first realms, Niflheim, the land of fog and frost, ice, and darkness.

Runic Notes
Isa, Ísa, Is
Date:
Time:
Lunar Phase:

What did the Rune(S) reveal to me?

How does this apply to me?

Runic Notes
Isa, Ísa, Is
Date:
Time:
Lunar Phase:

What did the Rune(S) reveal to me?

How does this apply to me?

Runic Notes
Isa, Ísa, Is
Date:
Time:
Lunar Phase:

What did the Rune(S) reveal to me?

How does this apply to me?

Jera, Ár, Ger

ᛃ, ᛄ, ᛡ

To sow is to reap
Giving joy to the soilage
The cycle begins

Pronunciation: Jera: YARR-aah, Ár: air, Ger: year
Literal Translation: Year, plenty, harvest
Sound: J, Y, A, Æ, Q, Ö
Magical Correspondences: Harvest, consequences, rewards, cycles, fertility

Divination Meaning Upright:
Jera, Ár, and Ger symbolize the complete cycle of the year. Everything that ends represents the seed of a new beginning. Everything that begins carries the seed of its own end. Jera, Ár, and Ger are positive runes, with appearances suggesting that the time is cyclical in Jera, is beginning an upward trend in Ár, and has hit the prime area of existence in Ger. The time has come to celebrate, for those who have made an effort to carry on a project or to achieve a goal. It is a sign of positive results for those who are thinking of embarking on a new business or starting a transformation in their life. The message is that, sooner or later, effort and perseverance are always rewarded. Precisely for this reason, these runes advise us to exercise common sense in moments of wealth, and to prepare, because at some point in the not too distant future, we will have to go through other difficult moments to enjoy new benefits. Jera, Ár, and Ger recommend seeking out wisdom, reflecting, and learning from our own successes and failures, in order to have more confidence in starting new projects or, simply, to face what life holds, for good and for bad.

There is no "standard" reverse interpretation, but as you progress in your path you may find that they show you a reversal of imagery or negative language. Allow the context of the reading and the revelations of the runes lead the way.

Delving into the Runes:
Simply put, these are the runes of the year. They speak to good work done well, and the harvest we get from said hard work. These runes are the origin of our modern word year. Jera, specifically as the 12th rune of the Elder Futhark enlightens us to how it coincides with the 12 months of our year. As we've seen with the runes before Jera, Ár, and Ger, like those associated with Fehu, Fé, -and Feoh, and the runes that come after, like Ingwaz and its runic system

counterparts, agriculture was paramount to the lives of the ancient Norse of northern Europe.[22]

These runes encapsulate the year but also symbolize the harvest, that which we reap at the end of the growing cycle. They can represent a cycle as well, and as we've seen with Hagalaz, Hagall, and Hegel, the harvest of agricultural crops literally meant life or death for the people within Norse communities.

Everything moves according to the principle of cause and effect; we reap what we have sown. Peace is not found in mourning, in regret, or in nostalgia. Death is no longer an enemy, but a faithful ally who reminds us that time passes and that what needs to be done must be done in the present time. Death is rhythm, time, and even as Nidhoggr gnaws at the roots of Yggdrasil, there is growth from that destruction, as they are tended to by the Norns.

---

[22] https://www.vaia.com/en-us/explanations/history/viking-history/viking-farming/#:~:text=Viking%20farming%20played%20a%20crucial,and%20rye%2C%20alongside%20managing%20livestock.

Runic Notes
Jera, Ár, Ger
Date:
Time:
Lunar Phase:

What did the Rune(S) reveal to me?

How does this apply to me?

Runic Notes
Jera, Ár, Ger
Date:
Time:
Lunar Phase:

What did the Rune(S) reveal to me?

How does this apply to me?

Runic Notes
Jera, Ár, Ger
Date:
Time:
Lunar Phase:

What did the Rune(S) reveal to me?

How does this apply to me?

Eihwaz, Yr, Eoh/Yr

ᛇ, ᛦ, ᛇ, ᛉ

Yggdrasils Branches,
Give us strength and confidence.
To brave these next steps.

Pronunciation: Eihwaz: EYE-wahz, Yr: year, Eoh: EEh
Literal Translation: Yew Tree
Sound: E, EH, ï, Y, Ý
Magical Correspondences: Invoking Yggdrasil, confidence, protection, strength, grounding, cycles of life, courage, desire, the liminal, acceptance

Divination Meaning Upright:
When any of these runes show up it makes for an interesting read. The Elder's Eihwaz and The Futhorc's Eoh do not have a reverse image or meaning. But the Yr of the younger Futhark does. What's significant about all three is they signify a time of change. These runes boldly proclaim that we will have to abandon ideas, beliefs, and lifestyles that have become old, that no longer support us, and adopt new ones. We see this concept most heavily weighed in Yr due to its connotation as a death rune. If we refuse to let that which does not serve us go, it will affect our own growth and future improvements, for ourselves and for others.

Eihwaz recommends not being afraid and awakening your desire for adventure, but also invites you to be cautious, and keep your abilities and possibilities in mind. Common sense and prudence are always excellent travel companions in life. It is certainly difficult to tear yourself away from what is familiar, however dissatisfied or distressed you may feel; it is frightening to not know what a new relationship holds, or a change of job or residence, and so on. But when you take the risk, when you dare, the satisfaction is immense and, whether you are successful or not, you will give your life a new atmosphere. You will learn amazing things, you will meet people who will introduce you to new environments, you will abandon outdated ideas, and you will feel better, more confident, and stronger.

Eoh furthers this point, brought forth by the courage of Yggdrasil, so innate in Eihwaz: Eoh is the rune of the bow, a rune of strength and longevity, a force to be reckoned with in its raw state as the yew tree, and a truly masterful and precise weapon in its final state as the bow. Wield it carefully.

There is no "standard" reverse interpretation for Eihwaz or Eoh but as you progress in your path you may find that they show you a reversal of imagery or negative language. Allow the context of the reading and the revelations of the runes lead the way.

Divination Meaning Reversed:
The Yr rune is the shape of the bow shooting towards the sky, urging you to follow your dreams and leave dead ideas behind you. What happens when this rune is cast or pulled and it comes out reverse? The bow is now turned towards the archer or the ground itself, either wounding us or burning any chance we have at getting what we are so driven towards. This is the result of staying in the past, of staying fixated when we need to adapt. This rune reversed is our failure to leave complacency behind.

Delving into the Runes:
The symbolic meaning of Eihwaz is directly related to the World Tree Yggdrasil, which personifies the unity of the entire Universe. The roots of the World Tree go to the farthest depths of Helheim (the Kingdom of the Dead), and the branches rise to Asgard (the Land of the Gods). Likewise, in the energetic component of Yr, we see the energies of Life and Death distinguished, and how they are in constant interaction with each other. Both are runes of initiation, into ourselves and our journey into the path of seidr, and entry into the Mystery of Life. The experience of life, positive or negative, forges the character and makes it unique, authentic, and capable of loving.

But not everything is rational and understandable; some things must be accepted for what they can be when they go beyond appearances. We see this in Eoh as we are called to heal the wounds of our soul through a journey between the worlds, through the various layers of consciousness that make up individual and collective reality. You must tend to the yew tree inside yourself. All three of these runes share association with the yew tree, which is similar to cypress, tall and straight, long-lived and resistant; it has also been renamed as one of the trees of death as it is often used in cemeteries and, among other things, and was used to create arrows. It is poisonous, due to its toxic fruits and fumes. Even sitting below a yew can wreak destruction on the body.[23]

Eihwaz, Yr, and Eoh represent the ability to transform adversity into something positive, the ability to always find new solutions to problems. As the hardness of wood becomes a factor once the appropriate use is understood, the difficulty becomes a tool, an opportunity to grow and achieve one's goals. By overcoming the fear of annihilation and death, one can come into contact with one's own inner strength. There is a lesson to be learned, a sacrifice to be made; it is necessary to die in order to be reborn, to abandon the old patterns in order to create new ones.

Due to the similarity in nature between that of the Futhorcs later added rune of Yr which references the yew as a bow I felt it prudent to tie it into this section with the other runes and

---

[23]

https://www.woodlandtrust.org.uk/trees-woods-and-wildlife/british-trees/a-z-of-british-trees/yew/#:~:text=Uses%20of%20yew&text=Traditionally%2C%20the%20wood%20was%20used,and%20used%20in%20modern%20medicine.

their meaning in this section as Eihwaz and Eoh both share the connotation of the bow, just not as heavily implied.

Runic Notes
Eihwaz, Yr, Eoh/Yr
Date:
Time:
Lunar Phase:

What did the Rune(S) reveal to me?

How does this apply to me?

Runic Notes
Eihwaz, Yr, Eoh/Yr
Date:
Time:
Lunar Phase:

What did the Rune(S) reveal to me?

How does this apply to me?

Runic Notes
Eihwaz, Yr, Eoh/Yr
Date:
Time:
Lunar Phase:

What did the Rune(S) reveal to me?

How does this apply to me?

Perthro, - , Peorth

The cosmic gamble,
To uncover or to not?
Be bold, dare to risk.

Pronunciation: Perthro: PER-throw, Peorth: Pay-oar-thh
Literal Translation: Dice Cup, Gambling Cup, Unknown
Sound: P, Pe, Pay
Magical Correspondences: the unknown, uncovering secrets, the cosmos or space, risks, gambling, to hide, glamour magick, Baldr[24]

Divination Meaning Upright:
Perthro and Peorth take us from the known cycle of life and death of Eihwaz, Yr, and Eoh, and rocket us into the unknown. There is little historically known of these runes outside the fact that they are in a similar shape to that of a gambling cup on its side.[25] And that's where the wisdom of Perthro and Peorth lies. Is what we're doing worth the risk? They ask if we are confident in our abilities to properly use the power of choice and decision that nature has given to us. They teach us to take an active attitude in life, avoiding falling into despair and blaming others for whatever bad thing happens. These runes invite us to be bold and accept the changes; despite the difficulties they bring, in the end, the effort will be worth it. They propose that we look at life with optimism, so as not to be overwhelmed by sadness or depression, which prevent us from living well. These runes promise that problems will always, in one way or another, be overcome. Perthro and Peorth ask us to look at the stars and wonder, "what if?"

Divination Meaning Reversed:
It may be that your energies and efforts are lost in too many projects. Perthro and Peorth advise you to focus on what is a priority, to decide what you want, and abandon insecurities and fears. If you don't, you can't proceed any further. Allied in this battle will be consistency and perseverance, but, above all, confidence in one's abilities and self-esteem will reign. If you believe in yourself, if you have faith in your projects and face the future with optimism, your victory is certain.

Delving into the Runes:
Though many rune definitions can seem straightforward, that ends with Perthro and Peorth. They are, in my opinion, the most mysterious of all the runes, and as unknown as the mysteries of space and the oceans themselves. Because of that, they are considered by many to

---
[24] thank you Iga for bringing this epiphany
[25] https://www.ragweedforge.com/rpae.html

be the runes of the Runes, the very key to unlocking the secrets of the runes in one of the few ways that we, as beings bound on Midgard, can. One of the definitions of Perthro and Peorth is the "lot cup," and many believe this pertains to games or gaming. The ancient Norse took gaming very seriously and felt that the gods themselves played a hand when the dice were rolled. Both runes can very well pertain to the act of tossing dice or other playing implements in the act of gaming, and this may have even included runes. Thus, this rune can represent the cup from which the runes are tossed, as well as the dice.

Many people believe that destiny is already written and that it is not in their power to change it. These runes, on the other hand, warn that this is not the case: destiny is the result of the set of decisions and choices we make during our life. With Perthro and Peorth, we find ourselves dealing with the value of initiation. The initiate dies and is reborn, they learn the mysteries and become the bearer of a new consciousness, they overcome the profane condition of the individual who, up to that moment, has ignored the sacred.

The goddess linked to this rune is Frigg, wife of Odin, also called Lady of Heaven or of the Gods. Frigg shares the Hlindskialf seat with her husband, and has at her disposal the abode in Fensalir, one of the regions of Asgard.[26] From the name of the goddess, various words have been derived over time such as fria, "a candidate for marriage" in Swedish; frja, "to love" in Icelandic.

---

[26] Rittika Dhar, "Frigg: The Norse Goddess of Motherhood and Fertility", *History Cooperative*, December 12, 2022, https://historycooperative.org/frigg/. Accessed November 13, 2024

Runic Notes

Perthro. Peorth
Date:
Time:
Lunar Phase:

What did the Rune(S) reveal to me?

How does this apply to me?

Runic Notes
Perthro, Peorth
Date:
Time:
Lunar Phase:

What did the Rune(S) reveal to me?

How does this apply to me?

Algiz/Elhaz, -, Eolh

As the Elk watches,
And the Old Gods protect
We too are kept safe.

Pronunciation: Algiz: AL-geez, Eolh: Yole-h
Literal Translation: Elk, Elk-sedge, Protection
Sound: Z, X
Magical Correspondences: blessings, defense, protection, adventure, invoking the guidance of the elk, liminal spaces, to challenge or adapt

Divination Meaning Upright:
Algiz and Eolh inform us that our prayers and words are answered. Algiz is a rune of blessing and protections inbound, and this is echoed in Eolh which in the Futhorc shares symbology with both the runes Maðr and Man and they invoke an image of spiritual augmentation. That they immediately follow Perthro and Peorth is no accident. Those answered prayers are saying that it is the right time to take risks and venture into a new project if desired. There is no reason to be afraid, as long as you take a firm stance and weigh the pros and cons of the situation. Algiz ensures that you will feel surrounded and protected by the people around you and that you will enjoy the benefits of a positive influence. Eolh does bid us remember, however, that we ourselves know our virtues and limitations best; we must therefore be alert to identify possible dangers in time, and not wade into the marsh with the elk sedge that these runes are named for.

Divination Meaning Reversed:
Reversed, Algiz's advice is clear: one must be cautious. If you act with imprudence, you will end up seeking some type of forgiveness or another chance, in one form or another. When Algiz is cast or pulled in reverse it states that you are surrounded by negative energies that hinder your path. The best thing, says Algiz, is to defend yourself against them, and not try to overcome them, until you are strengthened in body and spirit. It may also be that you are not creating the right distance from the problems of others, and that this is draining your energy. Algiz recommends understanding and helping others, without feeling responsible for their lives. This will also make it easier to help them.

There is no "standard" reverse interpretation for Eolh as it is the rune Man in the Futhorc if flipped (which may reveal itself to be the proper connotation in the reading), but as you progress in your path you may find that the runes in question show you a new reversal imagery all their own. Allow the context of the reading and the revelations of the runes lead the way.

Delving into the Runes:
Algiz and Eolh are the runes of the elk, or the elk sedge. There is no other rune that is better regarded for its protective qualities than these. These runes emulate the quality of the elk: steadfast, protective, and strong. Elk sedge is a swampy plant that elk (moose) prefer to eat, and it's a very thorny plant that can hurt you if you grasp it improperly.[27] There are strong correlations between Algiz, Eolh, and antlers, such as those of an elk or deer. Not only are these runes of protection, they are runes that insist we reach out to the liminal spaces, where the Elk and Moose tread, for help and protection.

Ansuz and its system counterparts represent the advice we are given, while Algiz and Eolh represent our ability to put it into practice; they are the runes that protect us from all kinds of enemies, if we only learn to create a sacred space around us and within us. Every time we extract one of these runes during a reading or we are left with a mark that is impossible to ignore, we must be ready to face the challenge that is proposed to us, without any delay, even if what we have to do creates discomfort and annoyance.

Odin learned the secret of the runes by sacrificing himself, wounded by his own spear, hanging on the cosmic tree. Algiz is the altar, the sacred grove, the temple, and the sacred space inside and outside the body. Eolh is the rune that can defend us from any enemy seeking to get in, just as the elk sedge harms those who are not careful. Both runes carry the lesson of creating around us a sacred space, a temple, an enclosure within which divinity is present. There is a divine spark that shines in every living being. How do we bring it to light?

---

[27] https://www.minnesotawildflowers.info/grass-sedge-rush/elk-sedge

Runic Notes

Algiz/Elhaz, Eolh
Date:
Time:
Lunar Phase:

What did the Rune(S) reveal to me?

How does this apply to me?

Runic Notes

Algiz/Elhaz, Eolh
Date:
Time:
Lunar Phase:

What did the Rune(S) reveal to me?

How does this apply to me?

Sowilo, Sól, Sigel

ᛋ

The start of summer
Time of the light and sun that
Melts ice and brings warmth

Pronunciation: Sowilo: So-WEE-lo, Sól: Soul, Sigel: si-jell
Literal Translation: Sun
Sound: S, X
Magical Correspondences: the sun, invoking Sol, energy, vitality, heat, winning, power, blossoming

Divination Meaning Upright:
Sowilo, Sól and Sigel are one set of automatic "Yes" runes in all three of the runic systems. All are associated with the Sun, an inexhaustible source of light and energy. They announce that you are going through an excellent moment in your life and that you have the nat-twenty to carry out the aspirations of your dreams at hand. You can take advantage of great mental clarity, and this allows you to channel your efforts well, as long as you allow yourself to be ruled by prudence, a gift that must never be lacking. These runes also have the power to eliminate the negative aspects that could be associated with another rune that came out in the cast. This is an ideal time to find solutions and make decisions that have been postponed until now.

There is no "standard" reverse interpretation, but as you progress in your path you may find that they show you a reversal of imagery or negative language. Allow the context of the reading and the revelations of the runes lead the way.

Delving into the Runes:
Sowilo, Söl, and Sigel all hold the claim of being the runes of the sun. They are the runes of solar light, and thereby lend themselves to being runes of power. For the ancient Norse, as well as many other ancient cultures, there was no power more respected and revered in the Universe than that of the sun. Sowilo is the last rune in Heimdalls Aett, moving well away from Hagalaz and Isa at the beginning of the aett; this is the rune that melts the ice of discomfort.

The Ancient Norse saw Sól (the sun goddess) as warm and feminine:; with the heat and warmth she provided, they again are runes of power and vitality. Sowilo means energy, life force, and honesty. In the course of divination, if any of these runes comes out, a notable vitality or an irrepressible spirit of enterprise is highlighted, that pervades the consultant.

They are the runes of blossoming that urge us to draw heavily on our talents, even if they appear irrelevant. There is also a warning against presumption and running out of energy reserves. In contrast to Algiz's defensive force, Sowilo, Sól, and Sigel as the ingrained force of the sun have an aggressive matrix. Attempts to misuse this energy will culminate in darkness and despair. These runes allow us to enjoy the warmth of the sun, the divine light that guides us and illuminates our life in every moment. We have overcome the dark times and great difficulties, we are free and light, but we have new energy within us, a new power. This power can be used at our discretion; we decide whether to use it for good or bad. Sowilo is the power inherent in matter; as the sun produces light and heat, so too can we use our surroundings to obtain power.

Runic Notes
Sowilo, Sól, Sigel
Date:
Time:
Lunar Phase:

What did the Rune(S) reveal to me?

How does this apply to me?

Runic Notes
Sowilo, Sól, Sigel
Date:
Time:
Lunar Phase:

What did the Rune(S) reveal to me?

How does this apply to me?

Runic Notes
Sowilo, Sól, Sigel
Date:
Time:
Lunar Phase:

What did the Rune(S) reveal to me?

How does this apply to me?

Tyr's Aett

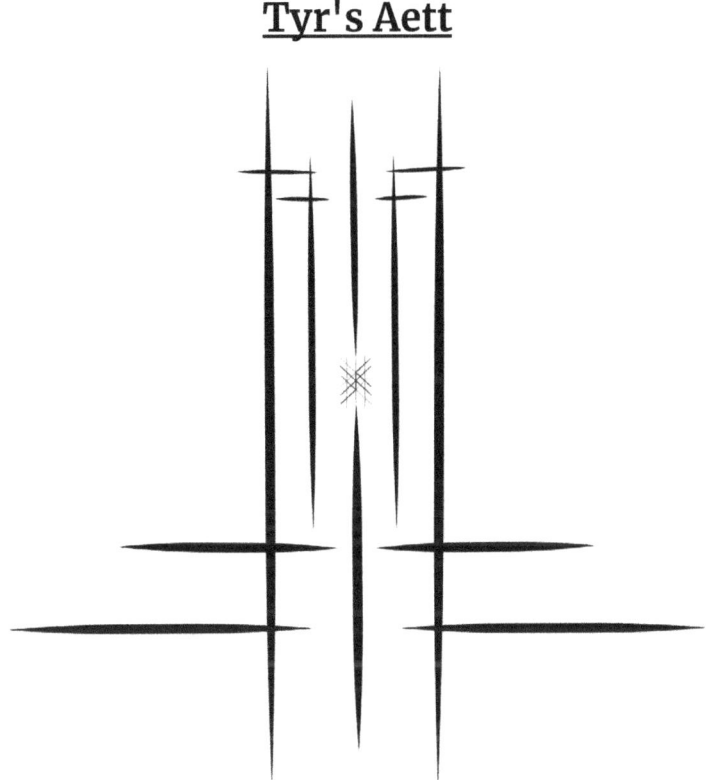

Tiwaz, Týr, Tiw

Honor and Courage,
Quickly, Bluntly; They will mold
Persevere and Rise

Pronunciation: Tiwaz: TEE-waz, Týr: tear, Tiw: tew/tuu
Literal Translation: Tyr, honor, victory
Sound: T, d, z, ti, tir
Magical Correspondences: Justice, Honor, Offensive weapons, Sacrifice, order, battle, Invoking Tyr, indicator, arrow

Divination Meaning Upright:
Tiwaz, Týr, and Tiw all advise one to act with honor and courage, and not always in grandiose ways. The appearance of this rune can also announce a period of change. Certainly, new projects will be started (change of job, home, etc.) or events will change one's lifestyle (marriage, the birth of a child, or moving to another country). All this indicates that it is time to apply the wisdom accumulated so far, so that everything goes in the best way. But it is necessary to be careful, to learn from all these new and promising experiences, so that no opportunities escape. Approach these changes with a sense of duty and order.

In practice, these runes can be used almost everywhere; their energies are positive, but require strength to achieve goals. They can serve as an indicator of the goal, or in contrast, they can be a means of achieving this goal. They can promise success in our actions, but only with some personal sacrifice. They also suggest success in matters of justice, if we are honorable and truthful. These runes are of justice, honor, and courage, so don't be surprised, if pulled or cast in a reading, that they are speaking of something which the client does not want to hear or accept at that time.

Divination Meaning Reversed:
The message is decisive: they reveal that important changes are on the way, but if you don't have the courage to take risks, and if you don't know how to use your full potential, you won't profit from this new, positive situation. They also warn to be on guard against fears, insecurity, and lack of self-esteem. Instead, it is necessary to be able to measure one's strength and to work hard to achieve one's goals. There is no need to justify, nor to feel sorry for, the wounds suffered in the past. If you want to live, says Tiwaz, you only need to look ahead and fight bravely for what you want to achieve.

Delving into the Runes:

Tiwaz, Týr, and Tiw are all runes of the Norse god Tyr, and we can best understand them by coming to understand his myths (that of Fenrir's binding and Aegirs pot). There is very little found in Norse mythology or lore regarding Tyr, but one legend that does exist tells us a great deal about this god. The most well-known tale of Tyr is the Binding of Fenrir, or Loki's wolf son. Fenrir was a wolf pup that was growing at a rapid rate, so quickly the gods feared for their safety. They entreated the Dwarves to make a chain for Fenrir with which to bind him, so he couldn't escape and be a threat. Fenrir, ever suspicious, would only wear the chain the gods brought to him if a god would put his hand in the wolf's mouth as a sign of good faith. Tyr was the only god to step up to the challenge, and when Fenrir was incapable of breaking free of the chain that bound him, he bit off Tyr's hand.[28] I implore you to read the rest of the story as this is just my paraphrased synopsis on how these runes' meanings connect to Tyr and the lore in a single facet. It is in this instance however that the runes of Tyr came to be the symbols of cosmic order, especially justice as decided by war.

The Ancient Norse considered themselves honorable, as much as they could be, in their pursuit of war, and oftentimes the day and times of battles were decided beforehand. It was a custom that battle could be averted by a duel, letting the gods decide the fate of the two warring parties by who they designated the winner.[29] Tiwaz, Týr, and Tiw, much like a spear itself, have been found in archaeological records etched and carved into spears and other weapons. These are the runes of all kinds of warriors, urging us to pay close attention to honor, integrity, and duty, and at times they call us to selflessly serve.

These runes can lend moral strength to those who need it, providing the will to succeed and, when used in combination with Sowilo, Söl, and Sigel, can provide almost unstoppable force. They remind us of the importance of upholding promises and oaths, and that all of our actions should be rooted in principle. We must be courageous in the face of adversity, tenacious in our pursuit of fairness, and disciplined in how we carry ourselves. In runic formulas, they can be used as a protective or, on the contrary, an aggressive rune.

---

[28] prose edda Gylfaginning Chapter 34
[29] https://www.vikinganswerlady.com/holmgang.shtml

Runic Notes
Tiwaz, Týr, Tiw
Date:
Time:
Lunar Phase:

What did the Rune(S) reveal to me?

How does this apply to me?

Runic Notes
Tiwaz, Týr, Tiw
Date:
Time:
Lunar Phase:

What did the Rune(S) reveal to me?

How does this apply to me?

Runic Notes
Tiwaz, Týr, Tiw
Date:
Time:
Lunar Phase:

What did the Rune(S) reveal to me?

How does this apply to me?

Berkano, Björk, Beorc

Birth of new venture,
From rich soil, and daring minds
Those called move onward

Pronunciation: Berkano: BER-kahn-O, Björk: bee-york, Beorc: bee-yore
Literal Translation: Birch Tree
Sound: B, P
Magical Correspondences: fertility, re birth, new venture, spring, abundance, femme energy, Birch, invoking Jord, energy and healing, nurturing

Divination Meaning Upright:
Berkano, Björk, and Beorc, when revealed in a reading, are heralds of great activity, in which one will feel full of energy and motivated to take new paths in the professional, sentimental, and other fields. The important thing is that all of this enriches one both physically and mentally. It can also be a good time to reflect on one's life and clarify one's true goals, so as to devote one's energy to achieving what one believes is really important: inner peace, generosity, and harmony in the family.

These runes are reminiscent of spring and abundance, and all the fertile nurturing energy that comes with it. They are reminders of and encouragement to perform self care, of regalness, and of the empowerment to make new and exciting things spring forward from hibernation.

Divination Meaning Reversed:
In this time of renewal, you have the opportunity to give life to new projects. These runes being pulled or cast reversed ask that you practice discernment and review your way of thinking and acting in certain circumstances. These runes warn that blaming others for your failures leads nowhere. Only by learning to recognize your mistakes will you be able to make the necessary changes. The secret lies, once again, in learning to know one another, striving to act consistently, and aiming at those events that will make you feel fully satisfied.

Delving into the Runes:
Berkano, Björk, and Beorc all translate to the birch tree[30], and carry meanings of growth, family, and maturity. Being runes that are often associated with matronly energy and fertility, they are said to announce a birth or a marriage; however, they can also be indicative of a new way of thinking, the start of a business, or the merger of two different mentalities aimed at

---

[30] https://www.ragweedforge.com/poems.html

achieving a common goal. This life-giving force especially advises the spiritual seeker not to exclude sexuality from their existence, as the path to enlightenment does not necessarily pass through asceticism. They are runes of purification, renewal, sexuality, death, birth, and rebirth. Their extraction puts one in contact with the reproductive mysteries, with the ability to welcome and give life, to nourish and protect.

We are making peace with ourselves by recomposing the fragments of the soul, preparing ourselves for a new spring, and the desire to leave the cold of winter behind us is very strong. Something new is transforming within us: a project, an idea, a desire, a dream. Berkano, Björk, and Beorc reconnect our being with the Soul of the World, with Jord, with a sense of completion and self-realization. These runes evoke a sense of humility, magic, mystery, and initiation. They are part of the spectrum of divine principles, of birth and growth, linked to the elements of earth and water in addition to the lunar energy that affects sowing, tides, and the menstrual cycle. They are in a sense the Anima Mundi, what is at the base of life, an intelligent principle from which everything is born: plants, minerals, animals, and everything else is its emanation, something from which we originate and to which we must then return at the end of a cycle. The shape of the rune recalls the profile of a pregnant being, about to give birth, with the breast full of milk and the belly bearing life.

The birch was, and still is, a tree much appreciated in the countries of the north; from my experience and crafting I have found that the wood is one of the most suitable for processing, the resistant bark tiles were obtained for huts, and small boats were built with the planking. In times of famine, flour from the rind was added to bread dough due to the presence of salts, sugars, and aromatic substances. The leaves were used in herbal medicine to regulate the metabolism and the activity of the exchange system; they move what is old out of the body, and they are antidiuretic and antirheumatic. They are a cure-all in the sense of teaching us to activate our renewal within.[31]

These runes are associated with those related to the earth and spring. Among these, we find the Nordic goddess Iðunn. Iðunn is the goddess of spring from Norse mythology. She belongs to the lineage of the Æsir, and is the wife of Bragi the god of poetry. Another we see is Jord, the Norse equivalent of mother earth and birther of Thor.

---

[31] https://treesforlife.org.uk/into-the-forest/trees-plants-animals/trees/birch/birch-mythology-and-folklore/

Runic Notes
Berkano, Björk, Beorc
Date:
Time:
Lunar Phase:

What did the Rune(S) reveal to me?

How does this apply to me?

Runic Notes
Berkano, Björk, Beorc
<u>Date:</u>
<u>Time:</u>
<u>Lunar Phase:</u>

What did the Rune(S) reveal to me?

How does this apply to me?

Runic Notes
Berkano, Björk, Beorc
Date:
Time:
Lunar Phase:

What did the Rune(S) reveal to me?

How does this apply to me?

Ehwaz, -, Eh

Rider and Horse
A symbol of harmony
Reaching their called path.

Pronunciation: Ehwaz: EHH-was, Eh: ayy
Literal Translation: Horse
Sound: E, Eh
Magical Correspondences: Partners, horse, power, balance, control, journeys, growth, metamorphosis

Divination Meaning Upright:
Ehwaz; and Eh herald the dichotomy of the horse's power and that of mankind's desire to have and control power. They are runes of balance and harmony, and if pulled upright in a reading they symbolize transformations and changes. There will be news and people will turn out to have key roles or will emerge from a crisis stronger, with new and more vital perspectives. As runes of balance, they beckon us to remember that we can only control what we can change, and to be understanding of what we can't. Sometimes we need to let the horse lead; these runes are saying to trust the horse and let it guide you.

Divination Meaning Reversed:
It is possible that you feel the sensation of being at a dead-end: it seems that you can no longer proceed in any direction. You're clutching the reins, yet feel powerless. In this case, Ehwaz; and Eh both recommend considering the hypothesis of changing the orientation of one's profession or studies, or trying to meet people from different backgrounds who provide new ideas and stimuli. To get back to a new set of basics. It may also be that you have set goals that are too difficult to reach; you may have to admit your limits are beyond your control and set your goals anew.

Delving into the Runes:
Ehwaz and Eh are the runes of the reciprocality between horse and rider. They are runes of partnership, cooperation, trust, and loyalty. They are symbols of symbiosis, of two separate entities coming together and hopefully creating a union that's more beneficial to both, preferable to an existence of isolation and working by oneself to make it through the world. Partnerships are relationships that should serve both parties equally, and any partnerships that benefit only one side are not truly partnerships, but relationships where one party gives up more of itself to the benefit of the other party.

If you've ever worked with horses, you know that they are to be respected and treated with care; you know that a truly proper relationship with a horse is one of partnership, not of dominance. If you've never worked with horses, you can still see this principle—or lack thereof—in the relationships around you. Imagine a horse and rider coming together. If the relationship is one of mutual respect, then both the horse and rider find themselves at their destination faster and with more precision than if they were each on their own. Now, if the horse doesn't respond to the rider or the rider abuses the horse, the principle of Ehwaz and Eh is out of balance and needs to be addressed; in this instance, the horse and rider should never have come together in the first place. Together, with mutual respect, the horse and rider are stronger.

These runes remind us of boundaries, where they are drawn, and how we should be clear in setting our limits. This principle of right relation is seen in Gebo and Gifu, the runes of equal exchange. Those who bring Ehwaz, and Eh energy into their lives are bringing the energy of Gebo and Gifu and their equal exchange into their lives as well. If there is a lack of equanimity, there is a lack of right relationship.

This idea of the right relationship, and balance between two parties, also applies to the relationship we have with ourselves. Not only can you ride others too hard, but you can ride yourself too hard, as well. These runes remind us to not allow ourselves to be ridden by those around us, whether friends, family, loved ones, coworkers, or professional acquaintances, but also to not ride ourselves too hard. Life is much easier when we become our own best friend, rather than our own worst enemy.

Runic Notes
Ehwaz, Eh
Date:
Time:
Lunar Phase:

What did the Rune(S) reveal to me?

How does this apply to me?

Runic Notes
Ehwaz, Eh
Date:
Time:
Lunar Phase:

What did the Rune(S) reveal to me?

How does this apply to me?

Mannaz, Maðr, Man

How many is the self?
In need of balance, or more.
Seek true self, one will

Pronunciation: Mannaz: MAN-naz, Maðr: MA-thr, Man: Maan
Literal Translation: Man, Mankind
Sound: M, MA
Magical Correspondences: yourself, the soul, third eye, balance, energy, healing, shadow work

Divination Meaning Upright:
These runes advise clearly focusing on one's goals. It is no small task and it could not be otherwise: it is about finding meaning in your life and giving it the right direction. Mannaz, Maðr, and Man indicate that you are on the right path, advising you to listen to your highest self and subconscious and learn from them, whether they are positive or negative. These runes therefore ask you, if you are a victim of anxiety, to identify its origin and solve the problem, and also to enhance what supports us, making us satisfied and happy.

Divination Meaning Reversed:
Perhaps you are at a time when you need to reconsider your situation; it is difficult to find one's "place in the world." These runes speak and ask you to reconsider the decisions and actions taken or to get rid of inertia. Perhaps you are doing something you don't like (at work or in study) and you probably need to overcome the fear of the new, and the laziness that prevents you from leaving the usual routine to open up to new horizons. It is enough to have faith in yourself and in your abilities to overcome all these obstacles that appear on your path, and which often are within you.

Delving into the Runes:
Mannaz, Maðr, and Man are the representation of identity, of inner being, our souls and higher selves. In Norse mythology, the three brothers, Vé, Vili, and Odin, come across two trees by the seashore. Vé gave them shape, speech, hearing and sight, Vili gave them movement and intelligence, and Odin gave them the breath or Ahma. This is how the first two humans were born - Ask and Embla.

Mannaz, Maðr, and Man describe the connections between people. They characterize a person as a representative of society, i.e. not the inner essence of an individual, but what they acquired under the influence of the society in which they live, all of which helps a person to feel like part of a collective. These can be roles that they play: someone's parent or child, someone's boss or subordinate, or a member of various groups, communities and associations. Roles prescribe for beings a certain style of behavior, certain responsibilities, and make them feel chained, dependent, or attached. Mannaz, Maðr, and Man are commitments in their own rights: a debt and a responsibility. These are moral and ethical standards. Finally, these are acquired habits, principles, and beliefs.

Mannaz, Maðr, and Man are the realization of the divine structure in humankind's increase in intelligence. When activating the dynamics of one's own inner power, or higher self awareness of our roles as co-creator of our own being, alongside both the gods and nature together with mental and spiritual potential.

Runic Notes
Mannaz, Maðr, Man
Date:
Time:
Lunar Phase:

What did the Rune(S) reveal to me?

How does this apply to me?

Runic Notes
Mannaz, Maðr, Man
Date:
Time:
Lunar Phase:

What did the Rune(S) reveal to me?

How does this apply to me?

Runic Notes
Mannaz, Maðr, Man
<u>Date:</u>
<u>Time:</u>
<u>Lunar Phase:</u>

What did the Rune(S) reveal to me?

How does this apply to me?

Laguz, Lögr, Lagu

ᛚ

Through ripples in the depths
Under the light of Mani's rays
Dive below and know

Pronunciation: Laguz: LAH-gooz, Lögr: Low-grr, Lagu: Laa- goo
Literal Translation: Lake, Water, Ocean, Sea
Sound: L
Magical Correspondences: Intuition, emotion, lunar, water energy, death work, invoking Njord and Ran, currents, power of the waves, rage

Divination Meaning Upright:
These are the runes of the deep, linked not only to the rhythms of the seas and Mani, but our psyche as well (appropriate that Rolling in the Deep is in my ears as I type this). Laguz, Lögr, and Lagu warn that the moment of transition is past: the time is now. Now is the time to listen to our emotions, the raging crashing waters within, and heed the intrinsic lessons·. Much like Perthro and its system counterparts, if we want to achieve the elusive concept of balance we are going to have to brave the unknown and let go. Taking care of our bodies will undoubtedly help us to enjoy greater physical and mental well-being. Calmer seas are ahead, if we implement the changes necessary to achieve happiness. Body and mind are not two autonomous entities, but they are in continuous communication with each other, and both need to be in balance and harmony, with each other and with nature.

Divination Meaning reversed:
Sometimes we get too preoccupied with chasing balance and with chasing our past, trying to carry it forward with our growing selves. Perhaps we are chasing a dream or project and becoming excessively perfectionist in every facet of the undertaking (been there). When these runes appear reversed it's a reminder to allow ourselves to feel. Feel the imperfections in ourselves, and in our undertakings, and see how a piece of us is carried in that imperfection. Those details make the project worth finishing. Laguz, Lögr, and Lagu are saying that the project (which is often ourselves, by the way) is growing and changing, and they suggest we adopt a more flexible and understanding attitude towards our mistakes and limitations. The satisfaction that we will feel for our successes, however small they may be, will have positive effects on our psyche. An attitude that is too rigid towards ourselves can, in fact, cause an inability to act due to the fear of making mistakes. Laguz asks us to be less harsh, and to profit from all experiences, both their positive and negative aspects.

Delving into the Runes:
We know the saying that water is life, and it's never more truly said than with Laguz, Lögr, and Lagu: the (literally translated) runes of the sea and the tides. In the ancient Norse world, travel was often over waterways, whether rivers, lakes, or oceans, and people understood how much water was necessary for life itself. They also knew the importance of water in death as well; waterways were seen (and still are) as liminal passageways to get to the realms beyond life. When these runes are drawn, especially with Raidho, Reið or Rad and Mannaz, Maðr, or Man, it can often mean a literal journey over a body of water. Water is everywhere: in us, in the ground below us, and in the sky above us. This is reflected elsewhere as Albios, Bitus, and Dubnos, the Gaulish divisions of the sky, the earth, and the deep. I include that, as they are part of setting my sacred space. Water sustains, and water moves. To better understand the wonder of Laguz, Lögr, and Lagu, we have to acknowledge both the physical water in our world around us, and the metaphorical water of our psyche, as well as the pull of the tides and how the lunar cycles can affect us.

These runes represent the ebb and flow of our unconscious, our emotional state. Emotions are typically associated with water, and the moon and our emotions are mainly part of our subconscious realm. We all have hidden springs within us, and Laguz, Lögr and Lagu help us discover them, whether in our waking state or our dreaming state, helping us to discover who we were, are, and are becoming. Whenever we experience heavy emotions, it often feels like we're "drowning." Many people who are overly emotional often refer to themselves as "watery," and indeed, tears are the water that springs forth from us when we are experiencing emotions that are too much for us in the moment, whether they're tears of happiness or tears of sadness. There are many expressions about water around emotions, like "Go with the flow" or "Keep your head above water." The connections between water and emotions have been with us since time immemorial.

Water is also one of the main five elements in my practice, the others being earth, air, fire, and the Ether. Just like these other elements, water cannot be controlled easily by humans, and if in enough quantity and force, it can never be controlled. Laguz, Lögr and Lagu represent the basis of organic life, for without water, life couldn't exist. They also represent the passage between life and death; after all one must cross the river Gjöll in order to reach Helheim, the Norse realm of the dead. [32]

---

[32] Snorri Sturluson's Gylfaginning, Gjöll originates from the wellspring Hvergelmir in Niflheim, flowing through Ginnungagap

Runic Notes
Laguz, Lögr, Lagu
Date:
Time:
Lunar Phase:

What did the Rune(S) reveal to me?

How does this apply to me?

Runic Notes
Laguz, Lögr, Lagu
Date:
Time:
Lunar Phase:

What did the Rune(S) reveal to me?

How does this apply to me?

Runic Notes
Laguz, Lögr, Lagu
Date:
Time:
Lunar Phase:

What did the Rune(S) reveal to me?

How does this apply to me?

Ingwaz, -, Ing

The great seed of Freyr
God of crops and Growing Hearth
The homes all prosper

Pronunciation: Ingwaz: EENG-was, Ing: EEng
Literal Translation: ing, freyr
Sound: Ng, Ing,
Magical Correspondences: Fertility, Family, Invoking Freyr, Harvest, Seeds, Anew, Secuality

Divination Meaning Upright:
The appearance of Ingwaz or Ing in a pull or cast makes it clear that an important stage in one's life has come to an end. This may mean that we are faced with equally important decisions, that we are about to reach a goal after long efforts, or that the right direction is now clearly seen. In any case, a feeling of inner well-being is being experienced, no doubt the result of these upcoming changes.

Ingwaz¡ and Ing's advice is this: if you want to break the daily routine without delay, introduce new activities and, above all, new interests that make you feel alive and stimulate your creativity (it may be useful to visit artisan workshops, attend conferences, walk in the countryside, or be with friends or family). The curiosity to know and discover new things will be an ally, as it will stimulate your receptivity, making you feel ready to welcome changes. This attitude will open up novelties that will enrich your life in every respect, especially as regards spirituality.

There is no "standard" reverse interpretation, but as you progress in your path you may find that it shows you a reversal of imagery or negative language. Allow the context of the reading and the revelations of the runes to lead the way.

Delving into the Runes:
Ingwaz and Ing are symbolic of the great seed, the runes of Freyr his older cognate, Yngvi. Freyr, brother to Freya, is a god of the Vanir tribe and in my eyes their leader, and was often appealed to by the ancient Norse for abundant crops and prosperity. Ingwaz and Ing historically represent the phallic energy found in the seed of the land, and of semen, and the correlation between the growth of the land and the growth of family. Both runes are still cherished as great runes of fertility. Statues have been often found of Freyr with a great phallus, and so made the obvious connection to fertility quite easy.

Ingwaz and Ing represent the very principles of sexuality, fertility, and expansive growth. As one can see from the very shape of the runes, one form appears very much like a seed, and the other like a DNA helix. Interestingly, they may be considered the counterpart of the fertile Berkana rune, and the two runes could possibly "slide" into one another, creating a union. Both represent the ancestral line as well, or bloodline. It is the great seed that gets passed down to us, and the one that we pass along to future generations.

To the Ancient Norse, we were all products of our family and ancestors, and our descendants were products of our lives. This is especially seen in the concept of orlog, a type of fate that is the result of a person's luck, but also that of a family. As described previously, the Norns are said to weave a person's orlog when they are born, and though it's new to each individual, it is also woven from the threads that have come before us from our ancestors.

These are empowering runes. Just like Berkana can be said to represent the energy of the birth giver, these represent those who bring forth the seed to be planted. We know from references in the lore that Freyr is a grain god.[33] Grain is grown and harvested, and then the seeds are planted to ensure the continual growth of grain. In this way, we can see Ingwaz and Ing both as the seed that is passed from generation to generation to ensure the successful continuation of a family line. Ingwaz is also named after Ing, or Yngvi, a great god known to be another name for Freyr. Ing came to be known as an ancestral god, or the Great Ancestor.[34]

---

[33] https://www.britannica.com/topic/Freyr
[34] https://books.openbookpublishers.com/10.11647/obp.0190/ch6.xhtml#:~:text=19%20This%20compound%20represents%20a,Ingvi%20(the)%20Lord'.

Runic Notes
Ingwaz, Ing
Date:
Time:
Lunar Phase:

What did the Rune(S) reveal to me?

How does this apply to me?

Runic Notes
Ingwaz, Ing
Date:
Time:
Lunar Phase:

What did the Rune(S) reveal to me?

How does this apply to me?

Dagaz, -, Dæg

Daybreak we succeed.
Adapt and overcome those
That wish to fault you.

Pronunciation: Dagaz: DAH-gaz, Dæg: Day-g
Literal Translation: Daybreak
Sound: D
Magical Correspondences: Winning, succes, daylight, change, joy, forward progress, a new beginning

Divination Meaning Upright:
Dagaz and Dæg symbolize daylight, clarity, transformation, and metamorphosis, a new beginning, health, prosperity, and balance: literally, all the good things. They are the runes of light that stand out over darkness, the triumph of good over evil, hope and relief. If these runes are cast or pulled, it means that there is a change taking place, and the querent is moving towards a positive transformation. The act is already in progress: the abandonment of bad habits, the end of a harmful relationship, the winning of a legal action, or gaining a new job, a new home, or a new life. This is the second set of the automatic "Yes" runes.

They are joyful runes, full of life and hope, which teach that to achieve one's goals it is not necessary to strain, tire, or undergo rigid ascetic practices such as fasting and deprivation. Dagaz and Dæg teach us to live with serenity, love, and tranquility. If you have a problem, and there is a solution, there is no need to go mad; if there is no solution, it's the same. If you are sick, you accept that you can and will be healed.

A simple lifestyle contributes to a life of well-being. Learning not to spend money impulsively and foolishly is important; with a conscience, one follows one's ideals. This is a lesson carried over from Fehu, Fé, and Feoh. There isn't a reversed Dagaz so each time you see it, it's in its upright position with this very same message for you.

There is no "standard" reverse interpretation, but as you progress in your path you may find that it shows you a reversal of imagery or negative language. Allow the context of the reading and the revelations of the runes to lead the way.

Delving into the Runes:
Many books and Rune Smiths place Dagaz at the end of the Elder Futhark system due to its connotation of a new day. This is not something I've ever felt drawn to. I see both of these

runes as a closed portal, and when twisted open to reveal its rectangle (or square, no judgment on drawing here), the open portal is revealed. Only when we reclose the portal can we go back home, to our version of Othala. Dagaz and Dæg both mean the day, dawn, metamorphosis, and advancement. The message that this rune sends is very important: only if you know how to be honest with yourself in dealing with your actions, will you be able to change your mind when necessary, or defend your beliefs and carry them forward with every effort until you achieve their purpose. Truth and light must be the guide of one's life.

Dagaz and Dæg are very positive runes, associated with the broad symbolic value of light (spirituality, wisdom, and energy). These runes remind us that life is a journey of continuous learning that leads from the darkness of infantile instincts to the wise harmony of maturity. Seen in this way, life takes the form of an exciting challenge in which, if you commit yourself fully, you can overcome difficulties and fears and solve the many doubts that cause anguish, until you live in peace with your spirit, without the influences of the judgments of strangers.

The appearance of Dagaz or Dæg reminds us of this. We are growing, and we are tormented by restlessness and insecurities. These runes suggest, however, that we continue without hesitation because we are on the right path. We must not fear anything, and must accept what life offers as a gift. However, we must understand that these "gifts" (friends, family, relationships, sometimes even an illness) are occasions from which one can learn to be better.

Dagr, the Norse god of the day, has the task of riding his own steed and illuminating the Earth every day.[35] Dagaz and Dæg are symbols of just that, illumination and liberation from suffering. This rune heralds a new beginning, a new era globally; it is the day after the night, after the darkness. After the pain and the loss, it is rebirth and hope, it is the joy of life.

---

[35] "Dagr." Encyclopedia Mythica. Encyclopedia Mythica, 3 Mar. 1997. Web. 14 Nov. 2024.

Runic Notes
Dagaz, Dæg
Date:
Time:
Lunar Phase:

What did the Rune(S) reveal to me?

How does this apply to me?

Runic Notes
Dagaz, Dæg
Date:
Time:
Lunar Phase:

What did the Rune(S) reveal to me?

How does this apply to me?

Othala, -, Eþel

Ancestors we praise,
For we inherit their gifts
Lessons to be learned

Pronunciation: Othala: OH-tha-la, Eþel: EH-thale
Literal Translation: inheritance, ancestors, ancestry, heritage
Sound: O, Œ
Magical Correspondences: Ancestors, Home, Goals, Realization, Legacy, Invoking Odin

Divination Meaning Upright:
Othala and Eþel proclaim that the time has come to concentrate your efforts on the goals you most want to achieve: a job, the love of a person, or the realization of a project. If you scatter the energies in multiple directions, you will not be able to accomplish anything, and you will feel frustrated. Perhaps this is a period of renewal. Getting rid of relationships that lead nowhere and starting new projects can be very positive. You must accept that life takes away some things to offer new ones. It is good that you make this truth your own to keep yourself open to changes.

Divination Meaning Reversed:
Excessive attachment, both to people and to material, cultural or social goods, is not a good counselor. If you accept that everything is undergoing change, and that losses can mean new gains, you will feel freer and will be able to live according to your way of being. You have to learn to adapt to circumstances and learn from every experience. In this way, you will make the most of situations, and you will not suffer when your desires are not satisfied, when you will have to face a separation (in your personal relationships or at work), when you will not achieve the desired success or, simply, when you realize you were wrong.

Delving into the Runes:
Othala and Eþel are the runes of family and inheritance, legacy and heritage. They showcase and highlight that to which we belong with regard to our family. They are runes that demonstrate that we are responsible for our heritage, both that which we inherit and that which we pass down. This is your lot in life, all the primal ingredients that make up who you are and what you bring into this life from your family. In ancient Norse culture, when a leader of an estate passed away, the members of the estate would erect an othal stone. On this stone were carved runes, describing for whom the stone was raised, as well as who raised it.

Othala is normally the second to last rune in the Elder Futhark, while Dagaz is last, but even when the day begins we begin it in our home wherever that may be, and may we always find our way back home. Family was of the utmost importance to the Ancient Norse, and should still be considered today; whether blood, chosen or found. To the Ancient Norse, there was no greater success than a well-established and abundant farm, family, and community. All of the energies of the runes lead up to this. Othala and Eþel show us that connection to our ancestors, and all that we have gained from them.

These are runes of inheritance and kinship: the clan stronghold. Othala and Eþel signify all that is important in loyalty to one's family and clan. In the sense of Othala and Eþel, this doesn't just mean family. It can mean connection to any group or organization to which you belong: religious, social, school, work, etc. In all things, we must remember the inheritance of the ancestors who came before us. We all come from ancestors who struggled and fought to get us to this day. They didn't have the hospitals, grocery stores, doctors, or any other modern conveniences that we take for granted.

This means we have a responsibility to ourselves, our families, and our communities to bring the gifts we bear, both to our clan, kin or family, and to the world at large. Othala and Eþel can represent the physical inheritance from our family, as well as the financial inheritance. It can even signify orlog, the luck and Wyrd that is passed down from parent to child. When Othala or Eþel show up in a reading, it is encouraging us to remember that which we've inherited, and to keep in mind the tribe or family of which we are a part. In all things, we must honor our ancestors by trying to make the world a better place, as much as we can, for our tribe and the world in general. To live a self-absorbed and selfish life dishonors our ancestors and their struggles; Othala reminds us of that.

Runic Notes
Othala, Eþel
Date:
Time:
Lunar Phase:

What did the Rune(S) reveal to me?

How does this apply to me?

Runic Notes
Othala, Eþel
Date:
Time:
Lunar Phase:

What did the Rune(S) reveal to me?

How does this apply to me?

The Last of the Futhorc

Coming to a Close:
In the next few pages we are going to discuss and take a look at the remaining five of the original thirty Futhorc Runes not covered alongside the others. I will be pairing these together as well as I feel that they feed off each other and bring depth to each others' meanings. This has been an amazing journey thus far and I'm ecstatic to have made it this far with you. Without further ado, let's dive into the pairing of Ac and Æsc.

Ac, Æsc

Oak and Ash
Thunder and the Wind
best times test.

Pronunciation: Ac: AHk, Æsc: aye-shh
Literal Translation: Oak, Ash
Sound: A, Æ
Magical Correspondences:
Ac: Invoking the energies of Oak and Ash, endurance or resilience, power, invoking Thor, compliments Ur

Æsc: Invoking Odin, invoking ecstatic state with Yggdrasil or the Runes, compliments that of Ac, speech or communication.

Divination Meaning Upright:
Ac and Æsc represent the oak and the ash, both royal trees of the Druids, and renowned for their resilience and strength. When they appear in a cast or pull they echo the lessons of Ur: you have the strength and the will to overcome whatever adversity you've been confronted with. Ac echoes with the might of Thor and is a symbol of having him beside you, while Æsc shares connotation with Os in the realms of divine speech. Speak those words and act upon them. It is time.

Divination Meaning Reversed:
This pairing is the best example of the reversed meanings among the Runic Systems that I've encountered. Ac and Æsc reversed represent failure and weakness respectively, ill timing and new found cowardice; look to the rest of the reading to garner guidance on how to remedy the situation at hand.

Delving into the Runes:
Through divination we can see just how similar Ac and Æsc are, both in their upright and reversed orientations, but what about their differences? What sets Ac or Oak apart from its other hardwood counterpart Æsc or Ash? We're gonna take a little trip away from the traditional runeology methods and visit some Ogham Lore (don't worry I won't take you too far down the rabbit holes - yet).

Ac or Oak in Ogham is named Duir, and carries the symbology of sacred qualities, great skill, and long life, and shares a connection with the deity Lugh as well as the Dagda, who had a harp made from Duir, or Ac in our case.³⁶ Æsc or Ash on the other hand is often associated with both ancient knowledge and that of the weavers. Nuin, as its Ogham name, is also associated much as Eolh or Eihwaz is with the making of arrow shafts from its wood,³⁷ and in doing so carries that symbology of strength and battle tested courage. Here's where it gets rather rabbity for us: in Ogham lore and celtic mythos, it is said that where Oak and Ash grow side by side the Fae shall live and play³⁸ (had to let some of the poets side out). How does this all translate back to Nordic Paganism, much less Runes?

Up to this point we have had runes be part of the laws of nature, and of the elements, and how they affect the world around us, but what we haven't seen is the representation of the Vaettir, much less the Land Vaettir. I mention the Fae connection to the Vaettir as a whole to get us in the mindset of really looking at the key pieces in nature and how they interact, to get us to look at the different Runic systems and find the similarities, but also find the differences that make each their own rune and entity. In the cases of Ac and Æsc, we see how their unique differences of skill and courage form a symbiotic relationship in the nature around them and in our lives as well. It is this relationship that is echoed in the very powers and elements of nature and the Vaettir. Nature contains these all powerful forces, yet the Vaettir show us something as simple and endearing as a dandelion blowing in the wind. Both come together to give us a sign, or to jog a memory, or give solace and joy. Therein lies the lesson of the pairing of Ac and Æsc: though things may appear the same, where do the differences lie that allow all to flourish just as nature and the Vaettir make the world flourish?

---

[36]

https://tree2mydoor.com/pages/information-trees-celtic-tree-calendar-oak-tree-symbolism#:~:text=Oak%20Tree%20Zodiac,Nobility%2C%20Strength%2C%20Intuition%2C%20Caring

[37]

https://www.learnreligions.com/ogham-symbol-gallery-4123029#:~:text=Nuin%20shows%20our%20connection%20between%20the%20spiritual%20world%20and%20the%20physical.

[38] https://treesforlife.org.uk/into-the-forest/trees-plants-animals/trees/oak/oak-mythology-and-folklore/

Runic Notes

Ac, Æsc
Date:
Time:
Lunar Phase:

What did the Rune(S) reveal to me?

How does this apply to me?

Runic Notes

Ac, Æsc
Date:
Time:
Lunar Phase:

What did the Rune(S) reveal to me?

How does this apply to me?

Ear, Calc

Grave and Cup
Both filled with those past,
emptied 'gain

Pronunciation: Ear: Ear, Calc: Cahl-ck
Literal Translation: Earth, Soil/ Cup , Chalice
Sound: Ea/ K
Magical Correspondences: Graves, Utiseta, Rest, Stopping, Finality, Relief

Divination Meaning Upright:
When Ear appears in a cast or pull, it carries with it a sense of finality: That whatever the query is, it is time for it to be finished. When pulled or cast with Calc this meaning is only strengthened: it represents the finality of the Younger Futharks Yr, and carries that implication of the dark that comes for us all. No, these are not cheerful runes, but that does not mean they are negative. There is a finality in the cycle of everything that came before, that energy and life can become something new. These are the symbols of a pit stop on the road trip we call life.

Divination Meaning Reversed:
Simply put: Stop stalling. It is time to move on and get to that final step of whatever question or guidance that was posed. There is no need to write more than that. You will know the answer when these appear reversed in a reading with the Futhorc.

Delving into the Runes:
With all this talk of finality, you may think these would be the last runes to cover, but alas they are not. If either rune gets pulled it can speak volumes if we only lend our ears (see what I did there). In the sense of Norse magical practices or Seidr, these runes are of utmost importance. It is due to this finality that we can go sit on the mound and seek consent for conversation by carrying these runes and asking those interred, showing we revere them and respect their rest, that if they choose not to speak we will empty the chalice and give offering for safe passage and communication back to whence we came.

These runes in my experience are two of the hardest to really define beyond what I have already divulged. They are blunt, honest, and do not have time to beat around the bush, much like those who we speak with from beyond this realm want to waste no time with small talk, and engage in real conversations. Many say necromancy is just divination through speaking with the dead, but in my eyes it is also the practice of keeping the beauty of death alive in the stories we can glean from ancestors, and the souls with a story to share from the veil beyond. There is beauty in finality, just lend those who have passed your Ear.

Runic Notes
Ear, Calc
Date:
Time:
Lunar Phase:

What did the Rune(S) reveal to me?

How does this apply to me?

Runic Notes

Ear, Calc
Date:
Time:
Lunar Phase:

What did the Rune(S) reveal to me?

How does this apply to me?

Gar

Yes or No?
Where to go from here?
Go forward.

Pronunciation: Gar: Gahrr
Literal Translation: Spear
Sound: G
Magical Correspondences: Alchemy, Sacrifice, Spear, Gungnir, Odin, Galdr

What exactly is Gar?
To put it plainly, it is the last of the Futhorc. To put it not-so-plainly it very well could be the first Bind Rune to make its way into the Runic systems. In my eyes, thanks to Kenn Edwards and their book Rune Walker, I see this enigmatic concept of a rune in a different light from my previous knowledge. That is the light of a door that opens and shuts. When the door is shut we see the rune for what it is in the most basic of representation that it divulges. Gar is a rune of sacrifice, a symbol of Odin's ordeal at Yggdrasil being pierced by his own spear. Gar is a rune of challenge, calling to us to open the door to make the same challenge as Odin's spear Gungnir flying over the battlefield. When the door is shut Gar reminds us of what alchemy looks like as it inspires our brain to tinker and dissect it - much like a Bind Rune (which we discuss later in the book). How does a rune or Bind Rune with no new phonetic or rune association or rune poem associated with it, entice us so fervently?

That my readers is the door made apparent; this is when we place our hand on the knob and begin to crack the door ajar. As we begin to allow the light to filter from behind this heavy door in front of us that's vibrating with energy, we begin to see the inner workings of Gar. We see Gifu and Ing, a pair most suited for what comes after adversity, Runes of growth and newness. After we note Gifu and Ing we see Calc and Eolh: finality and protection together. It's here we now begin to step across the threshold and we start to see a third coupling: Maðr and Tiwaz, symbols of the self, and of courage and honor.

With the entirety of our body inside the door we now see Gar for what it is. It is our awakenings, our deaths, our rebirths, our shadow work. All the times we push forward and sacrifice to make ourselves better and come out stronger, a healthier and better version of ourselves, we are invoking and becoming Gar. Gar is indeed a unique and fitting end to the shapes of the Runic Systems, and I challenge you to spend time with this rune and see what it reveals to you. Maybe it will give you a hunger for the next sections to come, to become a Rune Smith yourself.

Runic Notes

<u>Gar</u>
<u>Date:</u>
<u>Time:</u>
<u>Lunar Phase:</u>

What did the Rune(S) reveal to me?

How does this apply to me?

The Source Rune

Well y'all, we made it to the last piece of the puzzle in my practice with the Runic Systems. Bear with me now, as there is a major controversy surrounding the Blank Rune, also called Odin's Rune. What is it? The blank rune does not belong to the old ways, but if it's not a part of Norse tradition, where does the blank rune come from? Most runic scholars place the credit (or blame) squarely upon author Ralph Blum, who published his Book of Runes in 1983. This was the first textual reference to the blank rune. He was also the first to associate the blank rune with Odin, the most powerful of the Norse Gods. Blum divulged that the idea for the blank rune came from a set of rune tiles he purchased in England in the 1970s.[39] It's possible, some say, that this blank tile was intended to be used as a replacement for a lost tile.

When preparing to write his book, Blum scrapped the traditional (3 x 8 = 24) configuration of the runic system, and instead organized his runes on a 5x5 grid according to a random casting. The blank tile happened to fall into the final position on his grid, which he interpreted as an accident of great significance: a new rune for the New Age. Blum's books very thinly attempted to distill the dense and scholarly lore of the runes, (how it was viewed at the time) into an accessible list of spiritual principles, and while accessible it missed the mark for many, but somehow Blum's Book of Runes was still a huge seller in multiple editions. Its commercial success was due in part to the New Age and self-help publishing boom of the 1980s, and to the fact that some editions came packaged with a nifty set of ceramic rune tiles—blank rune included, of course. Among people who use runes casually for divination, it was often the first and only rune book on the bookshelf.

The improvisations in The Book of Runes caused outrage among runic traditionalists, and the blank rune became a focal point of contention. Norse reconstructionists charged Blum (and later New Age authors) with trivializing the runes and co-opting their heritage. But the damage—if indeed it was damage—was already done. A physical blank rune is included in almost every commercially-produced Elder Futhark set. The concept of the blank rune garners at least a passing mention in practically every book on runes published since 1983, though it probably only dates to the 1970s.

The above is the academic origin of the blank rune, but since working with the runes and embracing my path I have taken a special liking to the blank rune, which I fondly refer to as the Source Rune, after my toddler referred to it as such. It is oftentimes represented by the aforementioned blank rune tile; it is Odin's last rune, that the all-father has kept hidden. From this point the info following is my stated gnosis.

---

[39]

https://www.groveandgrotto.com/blogs/articles/whats-up-with-the-blank-rune-how-and-whether-to-read-it?srsltid=AfmBOor5gEF1zZFoXUejsv5D36vhRLY1CEsxt4wup5hdvPf4B_Eq3Vlk

The Source Rune is silence, the zero, the void of infinite possibility, the space between words, the breath before speech. Its Tarot equivalent is the Fool, the sensation of empty space, the Hebrew letter Aleph, the most primordial form of the element of Air.

The easiest way to read it if the blank rune does show up in divination is to advise the person who's receiving the reading to do some major introspection, and to focus on what possibilities could be told to them, as it is not being revealed to you at this time. Always remember however to use your intuition in your readings and to let it guide you and your words. With the belief that "everything has yet to be done," the Source Rune reminds us that we will travel lighter if we learn to give up the need for control and instead have trust in others, in oneself and in the generosity of nature, which always knows how to surprise us.

Runes are thought of as mysterious, as secrets, and the Source Rune represents the biggest secret of Wyrd in my practice. It stands apart from the rest of the runes, even as it has become a part of the divination system. It represents the X in the human condition.

My Rune Poem

What is wealth measured?
It's something to give freely.
Let all be gracious.

Primal and Revered
Will be great strength and healing,
Untamed with courage

A thorn or thunder,
Always there unrelenting.
Nature bides its time.

Poems, Prose, or Meter
Through mouth or Pen, wisdoms sought.
Paths not as they seem.

Heimdall, I call thee.
Protection, and clear pathways
Far beyond the Nine.

Inspiring through flame,
Creations find their shape.
Be wary of heat

Gifts plenty bestowed,
To share with all, who claim kin.
With this, reap honor

With joy there is pain,
Balance inwards to bring peace.
Cry, and you shall smile.

First of the Mystics
Urd, bringing growth from release.
The Well finds one's past

Duty to oneself
Paramount it is to heal
Present and Lucid

Glacial in approach
What will the Ice reveal now?
Patience proves fruitful.

To sow is to reap
Giving joy to the soilage
The cycle begins

Yggdrasils Branches,
Give us strength and confidence.
To brave these next steps.

The cosmic gamble,
To uncover or to not?
Be bold, dare to risk.

As the Elk watches,
And the Old Gods protect
We too are kept safe.

The start of summer
Time of the light and sun that
Melts ice and brings warmth

Honor and Courage,
Quickly, Bluntly; They will mold
Persevere and Rise

Birth of new venture,
From rich soil, and daring minds
Those called move onward

Rider and Horse
A symbol of harmony
Reaching their called path.

How many is the self?
In need of balance, or more.
Seek true self, one will

Through ripples in the depths
Under the light of Mani's rays
Dive below and know

*The great seed of Freyr
God of crops and Growing Hearth
The homes all prosper*

*Daybreak we succeed.
Adapt and overcome those
That wish to fault you.*

*Ancestors we praise,
For we inherit their gifts
Lessons to be learned*

*Oak and Ash
Thunder and the Wind
best times test.*

*Grave and Cup
Both filled with those past,
emptied 'gain*

*Yes or No?
Where to go from here?
Go forward.*

The Historical Rune Poems

Courtesy of Ragweedforge.com

**The Icelandic Rune Poem
(in Modern English)**

Wealth
source of discord among kinsmen
and fire of the sea
and path of the serpent.

Shower
lamentation of the clouds
and ruin of the hay-harvest
and abomination of the shepherd.

Giant
torture of women
and cliff-dweller
and husband of a giantess.

God
aged Gautr
and prince of Ásgarðr
and lord of Vallhalla.

Riding
joy of the horsemen
and speedy journey
and toil of the steed

Ulcer
disease fatal to children
and painful spot
and abode of mortification.

Hail
cold grain
and shower of sleet
and sickness of serpents.

Constraint
grief of the bond-maid
and state of oppression
and toilsome work.

Ice
bark of rivers
and roof of the wave
and destruction of the doomed.

Plenty
boon to men
and good summer
and thriving crops.

Sun
shield of the clouds
and shining ray
and destroyer of ice.

Týr
god with one hand
and leavings of the wolf
and prince of temples.

Birch
leafy twig
and little tree
and fresh young shrub.

Man
delight of man
and augmentation of the earth
and adorner of ships.

Water
eddying stream
and broad geysir
and land of the fish.

Yew
bent bow
and brittle iron
and giant of the arrow.

The Norwegian Rune Poem
(In Modern English)

Wealth is a source of discord among kinsmen;
the wolf lives in the forest.

Dross comes from bad iron;
the reindeer often races over the frozen snow.

Giant causes anguish to women;
misfortune makes few men cheerful.

Estuary is the way of most journeys;
but a scabbard is of swords.

Riding is said to be the worst thing for horses;
Reginn forged the finest sword.

Ulcer is fatal to children;
death makes a corpse pale.

Hail is the coldest of grain;
Christ created the world of old.

Constraint gives scant choice;
a naked man is chilled by the frost.

Ice we call the broad bridge;
the blind man must be led.

Plenty is a boon to men;
I say that Frothi was generous.

Sun is the light of the world;
I bow to the divine decree.

Tyr is a one-handed god;
often has the smith to blow.

Birch has the greenest leaves of any shrub;
Loki was fortunate in his deceit.

Man is an augmentation of the dust;
great is the claw of the hawk.

A waterfall is a River which falls from a mountain-side;
but ornaments are of gold.

Yew is the greenest of trees in winter;
it is wont to crackle when it burns

The Early English Rune Poem
(in Modern English)

Wealth is a comfort to all men;
yet must every man bestow it freely,
if he wish to gain honour in the sight of the Lord.

The aurochs is proud and has great horns;
it is a very savage beast and fights with its horns;
a great ranger of the moors, it is a creature of mettle.

The thorn is exceedingly sharp,
an evil thing for any knight to touch,
uncommonly severe on all who sit among them.

The mouth is the source of all language,
a pillar of wisdom and a comfort to wise men,
a blessing and a joy to every knight.

Riding seems easy to every warrior while he is indoors
and very courageous to him who traverses the high-roads
on the back of a stout horse.

The torch is known to every living man by its pale, bright flame;
it always burns where princes sit within.

Generosity brings credit and honour, which support one's dignity;
it furnishes help and subsistence
to all broken men who are devoid of aught else.

Bliss he enjoys who knows not suffering, sorrow nor anxiety,
and has prosperity and happiness and a good enough house.

Hail is the whitest of grain;
it is whirled from the vault of heaven
and is tossed about by gusts of wind
and then it melts into water.

Trouble is oppressive to the heart;
yet often it proves a source of help and salvation
to the children of men, to everyone who heeds it betimes.

Ice is very cold and immeasurably slippery;
it glistens as clear as glass and most like to gems;

it is a floor wrought by the frost, fair to look upon.

Summer is a joy to men, when God, the holy King of Heaven,
suffers the earth to bring forth shining fruits
for rich and poor alike.

The yew is a tree with rough bark,
hard and fast in the earth, supported by its roots,
a guardian of flame and a joy upon an estate.

Peorth is a source of recreation and amusement to the great,
where warriors sit blithely together in the banqueting-hall.

The Eolh-sedge is mostly to be found in a marsh;
it grows in the water and makes a ghastly wound,
covering with blood every warrior who touches it.

The sun is ever a joy in the hopes of seafarers
when they journey away over the fishes' bath,
until the courser of the deep bears them to land.

Tiw is a guiding star; well does it keep faith with princes;
it is ever on its course over the mists of night and never fails.

The poplar bears no fruit; yet without seed it brings forth suckers,
for it is generated from its leaves.
Splendid are its branches and gloriously adorned
its lofty crown which reaches to the skies.

The horse is a joy to princes in the presence of warriors.
A steed in the pride of its hoofs,
when rich men on horseback bandy words about it;
and it is ever a source of comfort to the restless.

The joyous man is dear to his kinsmen;
yet every man is doomed to fail his fellow,
since the Lord by his decree will commit the vile carrion to the earth.

The ocean seems interminable to men,
if they venture on the rolling bark
and the waves of the sea terrify them
and the courser of the deep heed not its bridle.

Ing was first seen by men among the East-Danes,

till, followed by his chariot,
he departed eastwards over the waves.
So the Heardingas named the hero.

An estate is very dear to every man,
if he can enjoy there in his house
whatever is right and proper in constant prosperity.

Day, the glorious light of the Creator, is sent by the Lord;
it is beloved of men, a source of hope and happiness to rich and poor,
and of service to all.

The oak fattens the flesh of pigs for the children of men.
Often it traverses the gannet's bath,
and the ocean proves whether the oak keeps faith
in honourable fashion.

The ash is exceedingly high and precious to men.
With its sturdy trunk it offers a stubborn resistance,
though attacked by many a man.

Yr is a source of joy and honour to every prince and knight;
it looks well on a horse and is a reliable equipment for a journey.

Iar is a river fish and yet it always feeds on land;
it has a fair abode encompassed by water, where it lives in happiness.

The grave is horrible to every knight,
when the corpse quickly begins to cool
and is laid in the bosom of the dark earth.
Prosperity declines, happiness passes away
and covenants are broken.

Bind Runes

The Background on the Binds:
You may have been wondering what those magical correspondences within each rune section are really meant for in regard to the use of runes. Besides Galdr (which is our next section), the next biggest, if not more prominent, use of runic magic is my favorite discipline of magic, and that is the Bind Rune. My goal in this section of the book is to answer what a Bind Rune is, how do we know of them, how are they structured, what can we use them for, and of course how do we make them. Let's start with what a Bind Rune is: **A Bind Rune is any magical formulation or ligature of two or more runes from the various Runic systems.**

This is a very simple explanation for what used to be a very simple practice. It has been formed by the historical and archaeological societies as a whole due to what we know from the finds of Bind Runes and other ligature works from the time period we consider the "Viking Age." Two awesome examples to look at are the Kylver stone from 400 A.D. (mentioned earlier in the book) with its repeated Tiwaz inscriptions, and the Södermanland Runic Inscription 158 (or Sö 158), a memorial runestone located in Sweden first in the 17th century bearing imagery of a ship and inscribed with same-stave Bind Runes to commemorate a man's promotion of sorts.[40]

Then we can look at our sources of lore. For our purposes, we will look specifically at the Sigrdrífumál section of the Poetic Edda where one of the lengthiest descriptions of the various kinds of magical runes is found. Unfortunately for us, the list does not go far beyond what the name of the charm or spell is, oftentimes just describing what each type of magic the runic based spell applies to. Another interesting facet, that ties into the relevance of needed shorthand, is that the majority of Bind Runes found and studied are almost never more than three runes, tending to favor the number two for simplicity's sake.

If we don't even know what runes the spells are using, how can we apply them? We look to what we do know. The goals of most Bind Runes actually uncovered from the Viking Age follow the usage and ease of shorthand of the Younger Futhark, and were used as a shortening of words, marks, companies and even inventory much like branding irons. There's also some classic examples of someone writing "this is mine" and having what looked like a Bind Rune next to it on a hammer or another kind of tool. Also to be perfectly honest I wouldn't be surprised if they were similar to modern companies logos or if there were others made and used for familial names and in turn legacy or memorials sake.

Why are they so popular and, in the eyes of many practitioners, running rampant? Bindrunes have gained popularity due to their intriguing blend of ancient mysticism and contemporary spirituality. They take the simplicity of the sigil and enhance it with ties to deities and cultures, and even provide a needed discipline within the craft. In my class "The Vörðr's Way" that I

---

[40] https://www.starkravenrunes.com/s/stories/the-power-of-bindrunes-in-history

wrote for The Fellowship of Fire and Ice, I describe the difference between sigils and Bind Runes as, "where sigils are abstract alchemy being brought to life, Bind Runes are the alchemy of the natural laws." The inherent agency the Runes hold to themselves have lended this definition to the craft of Bind Runes. They have become very much their own spirits, and as such I have taken to referring to them as the Rúnvættir (thank you to Sarenth Odinsson of Around Grandfather Fire for the term), and in turn they have gained a divine sense over the ages, from being used as shorthand to now being a complex magical practice in their own right. Oftentimes they are visually appealing, and beings believe in their efficacy for personal empowerment and spiritual connection. While opinions vary, Bind Runes hold significance for many individuals who integrate them into their spiritual practices.

How do we make them?

This will be the first time in my practice that I will be laying out how to actually make Bind Runes in a cohesive and hopefully inspiring manner. The art and practice of Bind Runes have always been a part of me, since taking up my path. They have been an extension and application of my own intuition, being led and guided by the Powers of Yggdrasil, Wyrds Web, and the Rúnvættir themselves, to bring forth those musings and inspirations that have become my craft.

When I set out to make a Bind Rune, I can be anywhere and be doing anything. When I create or transcribe a Bind Rune from an apparent claircognitive "divine download,", it flows from my mind to my hands, and with my intuition guiding, I allow the rune to flow forth onto the paper, sidewalk, tablet, phone, or even skin. These situations are not always pleasant: maybe I need to ward my car, or give someone healing, or someone needs a financial pick me up. Using the last example, I may hide a prosperity Bind Rune on a bank note somewhere. That's the beauty of Bind Runes in my eyes: they are every bit as free and unique as a sigil, but instead of feeding them your personal energy or channeling outside energy to bring them to life, Bind Runes are alive from the time you start planning them. The Rúnvættir's energy flows through your fingertips, as you become the conduit for an awesome and ancient magic.

This isn't to say that the only times you can create are when you feel called or are given a "divine download" of some sort; it is more of a way to describe the relationship that is required to truly make Bind Runes and not something that just looks like one. When setting out to make a Bind Rune in my system, you are agreeing to enter a partnership with the Runes. You affirm that you will respect, honor and listen to the runes you are *asking* to take part of the Bind Rune you are creating, and they in turn will grant you their energy and agency to help bring your Bind Rune to fruition. This next statement is not to play gatekeeper, and it is something I tell everyone who is new to divination, Paganism, Heathenry, or the realms of Spirituality when they ask me how to make Bind Runes. Bind Runes require an intimate relationship with the linguistic systems we call the Runes and the Rúnvættir. As spirits they are their own individual beings, and in order to truly work with them in the sense of making spells, charms, chants, poems, or Bind Runes, they deserve to be known as individuals, so if you are not at that place in your runic journey, I encourage you to further it, until you can answer yes: yes I do have that type of relationship with the Runes.

If you answered yes to the statement above the next parts are for you. I will be breaking down the making of a Bind Rune into a formulaic style to help build those bridges of intuition in yourself until you get to the point that you, like me, can be a conduit and allow your Bind Runes to take on a style all their own. I will break the process down into two main categories of multiple steps: The brainstorming phase, and the crafting phase. Before we get to that part however, let's discuss the different types of Bind Runes seen throughout history and why they still stand up to the test of time. It's also worth noting, I am self taught; using less than three runes in a Bind Rune was never something taught to me, or that one can't mix styles. This led me to develop a style all my own that has grown with me over the years. Do not feel that the guidelines and steps I bring forward are the only way to make Bind Runes, they are merely your introduction, a jumping off point for you to discover this world of magic, and to inspire you to find all the ways you can make sigils, Bind Runes, and alchemy in the most contemporary of ways.

There are 3 main types of BindRunes seen historically. They are stacked, same stave, or radial, which is a reminder or remains from the Galdrastafir of Icelandic magic practices

<u>All examples will be in Elder Futhark for ease of explanation.</u>

Stacked Bind Runes:
Stacked Bind Runes are the most common type that we actually see used. For a stacked Bind Rune, you take the runes you're working with, and "stack" them upon each other, making what appears to be a new runic shape altogether. These are mid level in difficulty because, depending on the way you stack them, hidden runes are revealed. Hidden runes are the unintended runes that are seen in the image of a Bind Rune after its final design, and an experienced practitioner will use those hidden Runes to layer the meaning or usage of the main Bind Rune. Stacked Bind Runes are most easily made by adhering to the less than three Runes concept.

This example is made up of the letters M (ᛗ), N (ᚾ), and R (ᚱ), which are Mannaz, Nauthiz, and Raidho. I chose these as they are the initials for the organization my sister and I co-own, Moons and Runes. I wanted to make a Bind Rune using those initials to reflect the type of space we try to foster for our members. With Mannaz were focusing on the soul and the self and what it needs, which takes us to Nauthiz: the needfire and how we try to help people get what they need in our organization. That brings us to Raidho: its all about the journey and whether or not a member is with us for a long or short period we want them to feel at home and that Moons and Runes is a place that is safe and that they can come back to at any time. This can be echoed in the generosity of the hidden Gebo and the healing nature of the Ur revealing itself on the right side of the Bind Rune.

Same Stave Bind Runes:
Same Stave Bind Runes are in my opinion the most common. This is because this is where most Rune crafters start building Bind Runes when they begin to dip their toes into the practice. That's due to the fact that you draw one main stave (line) and then place your Runes along that line in a process that executes your goals. Same Stave Bind Runes are most commonly seen as depicting names for phrases similar to the Celtic Ogham system, but instead of being read bottom to top, Same Stave Bind Runes are read in the orientation chosen by crafter. Same Stave Bind Runes have a bit more flexibility when looking at historical examples, with most being anywhere from three to five Runes on one stave. Even some of the ones I've done had (if I i-recall correctly) about thirteen or fourteen runes on a main stave.

For the purpose of this Same Stave Bind Rune, I wanted to demonstrate how different Runes would look along the main stave, so I opted to use Berkano (ᛒ), Ehwaz (ᛖ), Gebo (ᚷ), Ansuz (ᚨ), and Nauthiz (ᚾ), which spells "began." To me this word on its own is full of magick because of the fantastical stories of Arthurian times that started with "and so it began." It is my hope that this book serves as your "and so it began," when you recall your craft at a later date.

Radial or Galdrastafir Bind Runes:
These are in my eyes the most famous style of Bind Runes and that is due in part to the ongoing controversy of two symbols: The Vegivsir and the Helm of Awe. Both are important symbols in today's neo-pagan society, and Norse Pagans argue whether they are historical symbols or not. That is not a conversation for this space, but those conversations have made this style of Bind Rune famous the whole world over, and recognizable by almost anybody. What we draw

from them is the way they are arranged and built. Both symbols are built in a "compass style," where there is a central focal point, and the Runes used are laid radially using staves to keep branching out. This style has most influenced my own subconscious, and has been dubbed "the pretty snowflakes" by my kids and kin. In fact, it is a creation of this style that has earned the greatest compliment I will ever receive in regards to my craft. It was when a mentor of mine called me the next Skuggi, referring to the author of an amazing book on Icelandic magick, including some of the best Galdrastafir I've ever seen, called the Sorcerer's Screed, which was first published in 1940. Radials are in my opinion the best for spellwork and rituals, as well as coding multiple intentions and layering different goals within, making it a labyrinth of runic magick designed by both you and the Runes. Another key distinction is that when using a Radial template you have the flexibility to use other systems in conjunction with the Runes, either different Runic Systems, Ogham, Witch's Runes, traditional Sigils, or even Goetic if you are versed in those disciplines. In the example I provide below, you can see just how easy that can be.

This example of a Radial Bind Rune is designed for truth seeking and bringing justice to the forefront. To do this I used Tiwaz (↑), Ehwaz (ᛖ), Mannaz (ᛗ), Dagaz (ᛞ), and Sowilo (ᛋ). An interesting facet of this was the incorporation of the traditional Witchcraft symbol of the Pentacle, which draws on the elements as well. I placed Tiwaz in the four cardinal directions to show that everything will be uncovered, and the stacked Ehwaz amplifying from the base Mannaz are there to motivate the target to come forward, making them go on an introspective journey, and feeling all the things that go with that. Then we get to the center where Dagaz makes its home and the intersecting Bind Runes form multiple Sowilo, and Pentacles, calling for illumination and the elements of natural power to restore order to the land.

The steps in making a Bind Rune: My 2 Phase Method

The Brain Storming Phase:
What is your intention?
What do you want to happen, change, or accomplish? Why do you want this?

>As I wrote in the graphic build, I want to make something that brings the user and its targets peace in troubled times.

How do you want to use it?
Do you want this to be a drawing on a paper for a one time use spell? Are you making this to share with people? Will it be a tattoo? In all the ways you can apply something, it's important to decide which method of application is right for the Bind Rune at hand.

>I want it to be able to be used in a variety of ways: to be used on paper, skin, stickers, or just drawn on a surface. With both the intention and how I want it used, that means I need to formulate this Bind Rune so that it can be easily drawn and charged by anyone who wants to use it.

Where is it going to be used?
Essential to the process just as much as the how is the where: do you want this to be seen? Is it being used for glamour magick? Is it a curse on someone? Is it an amplifier that needs to be seen by all? Is this to be seen on your person as a mark of who you are, or to be put on materials to bring a desired outcome? The list goes on and on.

>The goal for this Bind Rune is to be applicable anywhere and everywhere that someone wants to use it.

With the other pieces of brainstorming in place, we are setting this Bind Rune up to be a versatile piece of magick.

The Crafting Phase:
Planning- What System, What Runes, What Style?
This really is as plain as the heading: you must determine which aspects of the systems you know that you want to use, and which runes you know that correspond with the results of your brain storming. Once you have answered that, then you have to try to decide which of the styles you might use, or even create your own style to be used. Experimentation is key to growth.

>For this Bind Rune, we are going to make it in a radial style so the energy flows in all directions, and we are going to use the Elder Futhark system for recognition's sake. The

runes to be used are: Mannaz, Nauthiz, Raidho, Dagaz, Sowilo, and Laguz (Think back to the meaning and correspondences in the prior sections of the book and make note of how or why you might do this differently).

Make the Bind Rune.
Now it's time to put it all together, draw, then redraw, then redraw some more, allowing your intuition to guide you. Make changes until the Bind Rune in front of you echoes with your intuition, the Runes, and your own magicks.

Charging or "releasing" the Bind Rune.
When we look at the aspects of charging and releasing Bind Runes we are reminded of sigil crafting. And we should be: many of the methods we use to activate sigils through charging and releasing apply to Bind Runes. Some of those methods can include: smoke, fire, dirt, bodily fluids including blood, water of multiple types, tearing, inking on different surfaces, or writing out the working for activation and release. The main difference is that we can "broadcast" a Bind Rune upon completion of construction by simply recognizing that it is completed and ready for use.

Oftentimes I build the activation into the Bind Rune itself as part of its makeup. Hiding the activation within the Bind, it is to remain inactive until someone who's not me draws it, for example. This is my favorite part of making Bind Runes: this inherent aspect of "coding" in a sense and structuring a full spell or ritual inside this now living aspect of Runes art and my own crafting. This is where Rune crafters truly find their personal style and discover the intimacies of Bind Rune making and why none, like a snowflake, truly are alike.

The Brain Storming Phase
What is my hierarchy?

To bring peace to troubled times
How do I want to use it?
On paper, sticker, or skin
Where is it going to be used?
anywhere that someone can place it.

Runes used: ᛘ ᛋ ᚱ ᛘ ᛏ ᛚ

The Making Phase

Planning: What System, What Runes, What Style?

to encompass the idea of being used anywhere, I'm going to use the radial style so it flows outward in all directions.

I will be using the Elder Futhark for ease of recognition, and the Runes to be used are:
Mannaz, Sowilo, Raidho, Dagaz, Tiwaz, and Laguz
half of the meanings and correspondences in the back price and make sure if you agree or would make it differently. Think about how you would apply the Brain Storming Phase.
Make the Bind Rune

So when making a radial Bind Rune I like to start by making my center focal piece. Because that's where everything's gonna branch off of

Then we have our final step where we add the caps to our staves so to speak. I decided to add Raidho's to the end of the caps to make the "signal" broadcast outwards and they then double as protective Algiz Runes.

Next, we add our compass style or circular embellishments of Runes In this case I decided to opt for making giant Sowilos go through the center of it as well as mirrored Laguz at the points to make multiple Tiwaz appear

Bind Rune Work Pages

Brainstorming Phase:
- What is your intention?

- How do you want to use it?

- Where is it going to be used?

- How will you charge, release or activate it?

Crafting Phase:
- Planning: What system, what Runes, What Style?

- Make the Bind Rune

Your Bind Rune

<u>Date:</u>
<u>Runes Used:</u>
<u>Name /Goal/Purpose of Bind:</u>

Bind Rune Work Pages

Brainstorming Phase:
- What is your intention?

- How do you want to use it?

- Where is it going to be used?

- How will you charge, release or activate it?

Crafting Phase:
- Planning: What system, what Runes, What Style?

- Make the Bind Rune

Your Bind Rune

Date:
Runes Used:
Name /Goal/Purpose of Bind:

Bind Rune Work Pages

Brainstorming Phase:
- What is your intention?

- How do you want to use it?

- Where is it going to be used?

- How will you charge, release or activate it?

Crafting Phase:
- Planning: What system, what Runes, What Style?

- Make the Bind Rune

Your Bind Rune

Date:
Runes Used:
Name /Goal/Purpose of Bind:

Bind Rune Work Pages

Brainstorming Phase:
- What is your intention?

- How do you want to use it?

- Where is it going to be used?

- How will you charge, release or activate it?

Crafting Phase:
- Planning: What system, what Runes, What Style?

- Make the Bind Rune

Your Bind Rune

Date:
Runes Used:
Name /Goal/Purpose of Bind:

Bind Rune Work Pages

Brainstorming Phase:
- What is your intention?

- How do you want to use it?

- Where is it going to be used?

- How will you charge, release or activate it?

Crafting Phase:
- Planning: What system, what Runes, What Style?

- Make the Bind Rune

Your Bind Rune

Date:
Runes Used:
Name /Goal/Purpose of Bind:

Bind Rune Work Pages

Brainstorming Phase:
- What is your intention?

- How do you want to use it?

- Where is it going to be used?

- How will you charge, release or activate it?

Crafting Phase:
- Planning: What system, what Runes, What Style?

- Make the Bind Rune

Your Bind Rune

Date:
Runes Used:
Name /Goal/Purpose of Bind:

Bind Rune Work Pages

Brainstorming Phase:
- What is your intention?

- How do you want to use it?

- Where is it going to be used?

- How will you charge, release or activate it?

Crafting Phase:
- Planning: What system, what Runes, What Style?

- Make the Bind Rune

Your Bind Rune

- <u>Date:</u>
- <u>Runes Used:</u>
- <u>Name /Goal/Purpose of Bind:</u>

Bind Rune Work Pages

Brainstorming Phase:
- What is your intention?

- How do you want to use it?

- Where is it going to be used?

- How will you charge, release or activate it?

Crafting Phase:
- Planning: What system, what Runes, What Style?

- Make the Bind Rune

Your Bind Rune

- Date:
- Runes Used:
- Name /Goal/Purpose of Bind:

Bind Rune Work Pages

Brainstorming Phase:
- What is your intention?

- How do you want to use it?

- Where is it going to be used?

- How will you charge, release or activate it?

Crafting Phase:
- Planning: What system, what Runes, What Style?

- Make the Bind Rune

Your Bind Rune

Date:
Runes Used:
Name /Goal/Purpose of Bind:

The Galdr Chants

What is Galdr?
By definition, galdr is a sung or chanted form of magic with a heavy emphasis on words and rhythm. Performed by both men and women, Galdr doesn't necessarily need words to be powerful. Sometimes when you sing and make up your own musical sound, it can affect things if you put intention behind it. Oftentimes it's likened to various indigenous throat singing styles. Galdr is extremely important to the Runic paths because of the power that is within the names and sounds of the runes; these can serve as another form of meditation, building that relationship with the runes, as well as becoming their own spellwork in your toolbox.

Starting the chants:
Once you have formed your foundation, you can move onto galdr. Sit in the dark, alone, and in silence. Hold the rune you wish to work with in your hand, perhaps paint or mark it onto your body. Finally, work yourself into a deep trance, a trance that feels like you're barely alive and are submerged deep below in caverns of old. Once that feeling is reached you can start. Begin by humming softly. Then slowly start to chant or sing the corresponding chant below. For these exercises I have decided to only list the Elder Futhark examples to serve as a basic foundation for the reader's Galdr practice and to encourage further creation and experimentation from the reader in their path.

While it may seem hard to find the courage or means to keep a straight face when beginning the chants it is important to know that our individual practices all have differences from each other. Adapt this guide to your style, if you feel called to Galdr. You don't need permission to experiment and find a way to enjoy every facet of your praxis. You can scream the runes from the top of your lungs as a battle chant or whisper them as you write, carve or divine with the runes. You can use the runes to help set the tone or intention of your own spellwork. Galdr is another tool for the toolbox that not everyone needs, but there's always more than one way to Heathen.

We will begin with Freya's Aett.
Freya's Aett Fehu:
Sing Feeeehhhuuuu over and over again: sing its title.
Then finally repeat this. Feeeeeehhhhuuuuu Fe fe fe fe fe fe fe fe Huhuhuhuhuhu Fehu Feeeeeehhhhhuuuu

Do this over and over again and feel the essence of the rune filling you with its energy. Do this until you feel that the rune has concluded its time with you and it is safe to exit the trance state. Exit the trance gradually and invite Fehu for its presence and guidance.

Follow this template for all the runes until you discover or find the way that works best for you.

Uruz:
Uruz uruzuruz uuuuuuuuu uuuuuurrrrrr uuuuuuuuu

Thurisaz:
thurisaz thurisaz thurisaz th thththththththth thur thar thur ther thor thu thathuthetho th thththththththth

Ansuz:
ansuz ansuzansuz awawawawawawawaw awawawawawawssssss awawawawawaw awawawawawawawawaw

Raidho:
raidho raidho raidho r r rrrrrrr ru ra ri re ro rudhradhridhredhrodh (rut rat rit ret rot) or er ir ar ur r r rrrrrrr

Kenaz:
kenaz kenazkenaz kukakikeko kunkankinkenkon okekikakuk Kaunnnnnnnnn

Gebo:
gebo gebo gebo gugagigego ogegigauur gaaafffff

Wunjo:
wunjowunjowunjo wuwawi wewo wunwanwinwenwon wowewiwawu wwwuuunnn

Heimdalls's Aett
Haglaz:
hagalaz hagalaz hagalaz hhhhhhhhh huhahiheho hughaghigheghog (hul hal hil hel hol) ohehihahuh hhhhhhhhh

Naudhiz: naudhiz naudhiz naudhiz nnnnnnnnn nunanuneno nudhnadhhudhnedhniodh (nut nat nit net not) unaninenon nnnnnnnnn

Isa:
isa isa isa i i i i i i i i i i i i i i i s s ssss (s s ssssiiiii) i i i i i i i i i

Jera:
jera jera jera j j j e eerrraaa j j j j j j j j j ju ja ji je jo (jur jar jir jer jor) j j j e eerrraaa

Eihwaz:
eihwaz eihwazeihwaz (iwaz iwaz iwaz) e eeeeeeee [a neutral, closed vowel sound] iwuiwaiwiiwaiwu iwoiweiwiiwaiwu e eeeeeeee

Perthro:
perthro perthro perthro pupapipepo purdhpardhpirdhperdhpordh popepipapu pppeeerrrthththrrrooo

Algiz:
elhaz elhaz elhaz z zzzzzzzz [a deepwhirring, whistling sound] uzazizezuz oz ezizazuz z zzzzzzzz (mmmmmmmmm)

Sowilo:
sowilo sowilo sowilo s ssssssss s ssooolll su sasi seso (sul sal sil sel sol) us asis esos si se su sasu s ssssssss

Tyr's Aett:
Tiwaz: tiwaz tiwaz tiwaz t i i i i i r r rrr tu ta ti te ter tor tur tar tir ter tor ot et it at ut (Tyr Tyr) Tiiiii rrrrr

Berkano:
berkano berkanoberkano bubabibebo beeeeerrrrr (burk bark birk berk bork) obebibabub beeeeerrrrr

Ehwaz:
ehwoehwoehwo e eeehwooo ehwuehwaehwiehweehwo ehwoehweehwiehwaehwu e eeehwooo

Mannaz:
mannazmannazmannaz mmmaaaaaannn mumamimemo munmanminmenmon umamimemom monmenminmanmun mmmaaaaaannn mmmmmmmmm

Laguz:
laguz laguz laguz llllllllll lu la li ke lo (lug lag lig leg log) ul al il el ol lo le li la lu l l l a aaggguuu llllllllll

Ingwaz:
ingwazingwazingwaz i i i i n nnngggg ungangingengong ongengingangung i i i i n nnngggg

185

Dagaz:
dagaz dagazdagaz dhdhdhdhdhdhdhdh
dddaaagggaaazzz dudadidedo dhdhdhdhdhdhdhdh odhedhidhadhudh odedudadud dddaaagggaaazzz

Othala:
othala othal othal oooooooooo oooooo othul othal othil othel othol othol othel othil othal othul oooooo

Runic Divination

When it comes to the way I read Runes I refer to the experience as the privilege to interact with and manipulate a small section of Wyrd. It is a personal and intimate experience between myself, the querent, and the Rúnvættir.

We can't have a divination focused book without some divination how-tos now can we? When it comes to Runic Divination, also called rune-casting, throwing lots, or even rune reads (readings), there are as many ways to go about actually conducting the divination as there are ways to name it. It's for this reason that I won't be telling you any one way to do it; instead I'm going to attempt to lay out how I conduct my reads, and if you choose to do so, you are more than welcome to adopt it.

At the end of this section you will find thirteen monthly read pages for you to keep track of any notes or interesting reads you may interact with. I include five spaces for Runes because I don't generally use the past, present, future aspect of a three Rune pull that has been made popular in an attempt to standardize Runic Divination similarly to Tarot. Runes are much more of a fluid discipline, and they will tell you how many need to be pulled, or if instead you need to cast all of them onto a cloth and read them that way (I do not read in this method except for rare circumstances, so I will not be going deeper into the casting of lots). The point being, often three spaces may be plenty, but just as often, three spaces are not enough for note taking.

My Style of Pulling the Runes:
Before I set my bag or box of Runes in front of me, I like to set some semblance of sacred space and set a tone that correlates with my needs for the session or sessions. Sometimes this is as simple as just speaking to my Runes and going into the read; other times I burn incense, don my red cardigan, put on some music and go through my incantation to make my space mine.

After I have set my space in whatever form it needs to take for the session, I then take up my Runes and I speak to them. It may be something along the lines of, "I come to you, the Runes and Rúnvættir asking for guidance, truth, and the knowledge that needs to be known if it be best for those gathered at my table." This is but an example and not always what or how I speak to them, but I always speak to them - we must remember that the Runes are spirits in their own right, and we would do well to respect them just as we would anything else.

Allright, so... Sacred Space? Check. Speaking with the Runes? Check. Now we are to the actual pull; it's here that I speak to the Runes again, as I place my hand into the receptacle holding my Runes and ask the query I wish to have answered. Then I wait, I let my intuition reach out to (and shake hands and hug with) the Rúnvættir, and when they are ready I let my fingers grasp that which needs to be pulled. I may grab all needed Runes at once, or I may need to go back and grab multiple times: **The Runes and Rúnvættir will lead you to what you need to pull.**

Now for the read. Let's say for this example I proposed no question, and simply asked for the Rúnvættir's guidance, and that I do indeed pull three Runes. I draw Jera (ᛃ), Ing (ᛜ), and Ear(ᛠ) reversed in this order. To better understand how they need to lay, let's jot down a couple key words for each Rune. Jera-harvest, Ing- the seed, and Ear-normally the grave or finality, but reversed we know that the time for stalling is over. How can we re-align the "spread" to communicate what the Runes are trying to say?

This is where the fun and beauty of Runic Divination lies. On paper, with no person to be read for, and not being a physical pull but a hypothetical, any way you orient this combo of Runes would be correct. Here is where we lean into our intuition and the energy of the person being read for. For the purpose of the example, I am going to orient them in the manner that first struck me: Reversed Ear (↑), Ing (◊), and then Jera (⌇) (looking at this now I think the Rúnvættir are telling me it's about time I wrote this book).

The Read:
Reversed Ear:
As stated above it is time to quit stalling and make your move. Make those first steps towards that goal, project, initiation, or dream you have been working towards.

Ing:
The message of Ear above is your seed, it is planted. Tend to it, nurture it and let it grow.

Jera:
When the time comes you will reap the benefits of following through with your desires. As long as you invest fully, you will receive back fully.

The Rúnvættir and Runes tend to be beings of few words and rather blunt, often using the least amount of Runes to convey guidance. In the example here, I was able to form a cohesive read from four sentences. It is not always the case, but do not be surprised when conducting readings yourself that you're not writing paragraphs or essays on what the Runes are telling you.

This is the most basic and general version of how I read. Many Rune Casters don't conduct their reads this way, and choose to leave the Runes in the order they are pulled, and don't read the reversed version of Runes, and that's okay. It doesn't make them any less qualified, or any less in their relationship with the Runes or Rúnvættir. We all do things differently, and who knows? Maybe someday you could be conducting intuitive Rune castings like myself, or even giving readings from your own Runic tattoos. My point being that, in the practice of Runic Divination, we are all as varied as the strings in the Web.

Monthly Rune Reading

Month:
Time Completed:
Lunar Phase:
Significant Days in Month:

Runes Drawn:

Notes:

Monthly Rune Reading

Month:
Time Completed:
Lunar Phase:
Significant Days in Month:

Runes Drawn:

Notes:

Monthly Rune Reading

Month:
Time Completed:
Lunar Phase:
Significant Days in Month:

Runes Drawn:

Notes:

Monthly Rune Reading

Month:
Time Completed:
Lunar Phase:
Significant Days in Month:

Runes Drawn:

Notes:

Monthly Rune Reading

Month:
Time Completed:
Lunar Phase:
Significant Days in Month:

Runes Drawn:

Notes:

Monthly Rune Reading

Month:
Time Completed:
Lunar Phase:
Significant Days in Month:

Runes Drawn:

Notes:

Monthly Rune Reading

Month:
Time Completed:
Lunar Phase:
Significant Days in Month:

Runes Drawn:

Notes:

Monthly Rune Reading

Month:
Time Completed:
Lunar Phase:
Significant Days in Month:

Runes Drawn:

☐ ☐ ☐ ☐ ☐

Notes:

Monthly Rune Reading

Month:
Time Completed:
Lunar Phase:
Significant Days in Month:

Runes Drawn:

Notes:

Monthly Rune Reading

Month:
Time Completed:
Lunar Phase:
Significant Days in Month:

Runes Drawn:

Notes:

Monthly Rune Reading

Month:
Time Completed:
Lunar Phase:
Significant Days in Month:

Runes Drawn:

Notes:

Monthly Rune Reading

Month:
Time Completed:
Lunar Phase:
Significant Days in Month:

Runes Drawn:

Notes:

Monthly Rune Reading

Month:
Time Completed:
Lunar Phase:
Significant Days in Month:

Runes Drawn:

Notes:

The Runes: A Recount

These three Runic Systems are some of the most sought after, studied, and used systems of magic, culture, and history in the world, constantly being referenced in media through video games and movies, and serving as inspiration for some of the best selling books of all time (if ya know, ya know). But even with all this exposure, somehow we still lose sight of the magic and the importance of the runes and why they're so iconic in the first place.

Effective use of the runes requires both the old wisdom and the new. We live in a global culture, and when an archetype from another land seems to illuminate some aspect of a rune's meaning, it deserves consideration. The Elder Futhark first came to be as the alphabet system for the teutonic and Germanic peoples from the Lepontic Runes of the Etruscans,[41] and alongside the Futhorc having reigned in early England well before and into what historians now call the Viking age. That's when Younger Futhark was developed and reigned supreme, around the coming of the tenth century.

The word "Rune" itself means "Rist" (to carve, or mark) and they were often carved into personal objects or property to designate ownership, or to imbue those items with the magic of the Runes. However, unlike other alphabets, each rune has a name derived from the runic poems, some of which we know and have collected through history, as well as their claimed phonetic values at the time of recording. I do appreciate and respect the nature of the given names or sounds of the runes as they stand today, as we have really only been able to piece together their current values and sounds based on etymologists' and historians' research into the archaeology of the Teutonic peoples.

Aside from the mundane aspects of the three Runic Systems, each rune also has an arcane or esoteric quality or meaning associated with it that can be invoked through the magical practice of seidr, as well as inscribing the runes or with galdr. There are scholars that reject any claim that the runes do in fact have arcane capabilities, and it reminds me of Stanza 144 in the Havamal:

> *"Know how to carve them, know how to read them, know how to stain them, know how to wield them, know how to ask them, know how to bloody them, know how to send them, know how to sacrifice them."*
> *(Havamal 144, Carolyne Larrington)*

This to me begs the question how many of the scholars have seen this verse, and attempted to live out their path with the spirits of the Runes? I would like to end this part of my journey alongside you with this reminder: The Rúnvættir are their own powerful beings, with an energy and agency all their own imbued in the Runes, and can speak unknown tales to us if we

---

[41] https://www.britannica.com/topic/runic-alphabet

only take the time to listen. No one's path or craft looks identical to another's. Your craft is your own, don't let anyone dictate or gate-keep you from the knowledge and topics you may seek in any part of your life. Meditation and study will take you only so far on this path. To walk the "Way of the Runes," you must experience the runes as they manifest, both in the part of Midgard that lies outside yourself, and in the worlds within. There are so many great written works regarding the Runes in all facets, whether esoteric, scholarly, or even in art. This book is not intended to be the one, true, and only approach to runelore, but a reference book to carry and help with your individual study of the runes, a blend of my personal praxis and gnosis, as well as history and knowledge gleaned from these amazing beings: The Runes.

Meet the Author

Liagis is a multifaceted individual who embraces various roles, with a primary focus on being an exemplary partner and parent to their wife and three children.

In the areas of esotericism and the occult, Liagis finds both joy and a certain expertise. They have established themselves through a unique journey as a devotee of Wyrd and the Runes, and their dedication to deities Hel and Heimdall have further enriched this path. Additionally, Liagis has developed several distinct styles of divination and continues to have a pivotal role in creating the new Sacred Role of the Vörðr in Heathenry for The Fellowship of Fire and Ice. They are also recognized as an eddic and skaldic poet, with various works published in Ancient Norse meters.

With regard to the Runes, Liagis has cultivated a deep connection over many years, continually exploring innovative ways to apply their knowledge. They have dedicated the past two years to perfecting their craft of Bind Runes, integrating principles from alchemy, traditional witchcraft, folk magic, and various forms of sigil craft into their own distinctive interpretation of Bind Rune Mysticism.

Beyond their involvement with Runes and The Fellowship of Fire and Ice, Liagis is a co-founder of Moons and Runes, a non-profit organization that aims to create a welcoming environment for marginalized individuals, including members of the LGBTQ+ community, neurodivergent individuals, disabled persons, and otherkin. The organization is dedicated to celebrating diversity and providing a safe space for those who may feel excluded.

Liagis views themselves as a lifelong learner and is committed to personal and communal growth, continuously seeking opportunities to learn, teach, and foster deeper connections with Wyrd, the Runes, and the divine.

www.ingramcontent.com/pod-product-compliance
Lightning Source LLC
Chambersburg PA
CBHW020929090426
42736CB00010B/1080